W9-ARG-514

Opportunities in European Financial Services

ABOUT SPICERS CENTRE FOR EUROPE

This book has been produced by Spicers Centre for Europe, a new subsidiary of Spicer & Oppenheim International, a worldwide accounting, tax, and management consulting firm.

The Centre offers comprehensive information and advisory services to clients throughout Europe, the United States, and beyond, on all matters relating to the European Community (EC).

By means of Spicers' own database, Spicers Centre for Europe provides up-to-the-minute information on an enormous range of European subjects, including legislation, proposals, new initiatives, grant regimes, and research programs. Highly trained information officers notify clients of changes that are specifically relevant to their interests.

Additional support is provided by a team of experienced consultants who are able to offer further guidance and to assist clients in identifying actual and potential interactions between their activities and the EC.

Important contributions were made to the production of this book by Spicers Consulting Group (SCG), the consulting arm of Spicer & Oppenheim. SCG employs over 50 professional staff members in its London and Manchester offices. SCG's experienced consultants offer expert business and management consulting services, drawing on an extensive specialist range and an impressive track record.

Spicer & Oppenheim International has more than 250 offices in over 55 countries.

Opportunities in European Financial Services

1992 and Beyond

Spicers Centre for Europe

Edited by

PAUL QUANTOCK

JOHN WILEY & SONS
New York • Chichester • Brisbane
Toronto • Singapore

Library of Congress Cataloging in Publication Data

Opportunities in European financial services : 1992 and beyond /
edited by Paul Quantock (Spicers Centre for Europe).
p. cm.
Includes bibliographical references.
ISBN 0-471-52213-9
1. Financial services industry—European Economic Community countries. I. Quantock, Paul. II. Spicers Centre for Europe.
HG186.E9066 1990
332.1'094—dc20 90-31157

Printed in the United States of America

10 9 8 7 6 5 4 3 2 1

Preface

This book provides a factual account of the proposals to create a single European market for financial services within the twelve Member States of the European Community (EC). In setting out to achieve that goal, the writers believed that they had two missions: to set these measures and proposals in the context of the entire process of the creation of a single European market for 1992 and beyond, and to present the information with an eye to the major political and economic changes and developments that currently dominate the strategic economic situation in Europe. To this end, Chapter 1 paints the political and economic landscape of Europe on a broad canvas, thereby offering just such a strategic perspective.

To suggest that a single European market is the brainchild of the European Community would be an error. The concept is the natural consequence of international economic growth. The international nature of economic development, particularly since the end of the recession in 1982, has dominated national economies. Within Europe the complexities of many different markets, currencies, fiscal policies, and other regulations have been an ever more serious liability, in the face of the giant economies of the United States and Japan. Thus the great awakening in Europe is both economic and political and has engendered the birth of a new context within which the institutions of the European Community seek to develop and implement the policies of the Member States.

Following the initial chapter's strategic backdrop is a more focused overview of 1992 and the creation of a single European market. The institutions and system of operation of the European Community are described in Chapter 3. Chapters 5 through 10 cover the primary focus of the book: the specific measures being implemented by the EC to establish a genuine single European market in insurance, banking, and other financial services. The final chapter assesses how the European Community is viewed from the outside. Relevant research and reference information is contained in the appendixes.

The book ranges, therefore, from a very broad overview of momentous historical events that are reshaping Europe, to the minute details of specific measures, for example, in the creation of a standardized system for electronic transfer of funds at a point of sale. The writers make no apology for this coverage and have deliberately drawn on expertise not only from Spicers Centre for Europe, but from other key divisions within Spicer & Oppenheim International, particularly Spicers Consulting Group. To move forward in Europe during the 1990s will require planning and preparation that are based on understanding. This book should prove both a thought-provoking stimulus and a valuable information source to all those in the financial services sector who are genuinely interested in coming to grips with a single European market and its implications.

Every effort has been made to ensure that the contents of this publication are accurate. The reader should recognize, however, that the subject area is a complex one and the contents should not be relied upon in individual cases; independent professional advice should always be sought before any action is taken.

A book on topics as diverse and complex as a single European market, financial services, and 1992, by its very nature draws on the expertise and resources of many people within an organization. A few individuals, however, have made a particularly important contribution. Anne Campbell at Spicers Centre for Europe compiled and wrote the substantive chapters on the proposals and directives, keeping track of a multitude of items as they made their way through the complexities of the European Community's decision-making process. Joe Egerton of Spicers Consulting Group provided the opening chapter on the strategic backdrop to business opportunities in a changing Europe. This task was not made any easier by the enormous political changes that have been taking place in Europe since October 1989. Alan Wallace wrote the final chapter and attempted to impose some continuity on a text that of necessity includes both broad overview and specific detail. Finally, Michelle Huby demonstrated both competence and patience in typing the many drafts of a difficult manuscript.

SPICERS CENTRE FOR EUROPE

April 1990

Contents

List of Abbreviations

Acronym	
BC-NET	Business Cooperation Network
CBI	Confederation of British Industry
CEDEFOP	European Center for the Development of Vocational Training
CEN	European Committee for Standardization (the acronym is based on the French title)
CENELEC	European Committee for Electrotechnical Standardization (the acronym is based on the French title)
COM	Commission Documents
COREPER	Committee of Permanent Representatives
DG	Directorates-General; departments of the European Commission
EBA	European Banking Association
EC	European Community. Taken to mean all three Communities: EEC, ECSC, and EURATOM.
ECOFIN	European Community Council of Economic and Finance Ministers
ECOSOC	Economic and Social Committee of the European Community
ECSC	European Coal and Steel Community

Acronym	
ECU	European Currency Unit
EDF	European Development Fund
EEC	European Economic Community. Sometimes used interchangeably with EC.
EFTA	European Free Trade Association
EFTPOS	Electronic Funds Transfer at Point of Sale
EIB	European Investment Bank
EMS	European Monetary System
EMU	Economic and Monetary Union
EP	European Parliament
ERDF	European Regional Development Fund
ERM	Exchange rate mechanism of the EMS. ERM is sometimes referred to as "the snake."
ESCB	European System of Central Banks
ESF	European Social Fund
EURATOM	European Atomic Energy Community
GATT	General Agreement on Tariffs and Trade
MECU	Million ECUs
MEP	Member of the European Parliament
OECD	Organization for Economic Cooperation and Development
OJ	Official Journal (of the European Community)
OOPEC	Office of Official Publications of the European Communities
SAD	Single Administrative Document. A one-page form, in use throughout the EC, covering all customs and excise formalities in import/export.
SEM	The Single European Market
SEA	The Single European Act
SME	Small and medium size enterprise
UCITS	Undertaking for Collective Investment in Transferable Securities (unit trusts)
VAT	Value-Added tax

THE CAPITAL ADEQUACY PROPOSAL

As this book was going to print the Commission approved the final version of the proposal for a Directive which will set out the minimum capital requirements for investment firms wishing to obtain the single European "passport" to operate EC-wide from 1993. At the time we went to press, however, the official text was not yet publicly available since the Commission had still to present its Capital Adequacy Proposal to the Council.

It appears that the agreed upon version of the proposal, reached after 18 months of negotiations, does not differ significantly from an earlier draft produced in February 1990. Following an active lobbying campaign led by the UK, the capital adequacy provisions agreed upon by the Commission were made considerably more flexible than those proposed in previous drafts. A brief outline of those key provisions that are expected to be contained in the final published proposal follows.

Initial Capital

Initial capital requirements for investment firms will be set at three levels: investment firms will be required to have a minimum initial capital of 500,000 ECU, but Member States will be able to reduce this amount to 50,000 ECU for firms which are not authorized to handle clients' monies or securities or which do not engage in market making or underwriting. A lower initial capital requirement of 100,000 ECU may also be set for brokers which act as agents but do not take positions themselves. Firms engaged purely in the business of supplying investment advice are expected to be exempted from the capital requirements.

Provision Against Risks

The capital adequacy directive will also set out highly technical and detailed rules requiring investment firms to provide capital to cover a range of risks associated with various investment activities. The methods for calculating the following categories of risk are outlined in a series of annexes to the proposal:

- Position risk
- Counterparty/settlement risk
- Foreign exchange risk
- Other risks

Some allowance will be made for hedging, diversification, offsetting convertibles against underlying equity and off-balance sheet transactions will also be taken into account.

Banks

Member States may require credit institutions engaging in securities activities to meet the capital requirements set out in the Solvency Ratios Directive (see p. 82). Alternatively they will have the option of allowing banks to calculate their trading risks separately under the more flexible rules contained in the capital adequacy directive. The aim is to provide a "level playing field" for banks and securities houses to ensure that banks and nonbank investment firms are subject to broadly equivalent capital requirements. This second alternative has been introduced to counter complaints, mainly from West Germany, that banks carrying out investment activities would be placed at a competitive disadvantage compared to nonbank investment firms because of being obliged to calculate their trading risks under the more stringent banking solvency rules of the Solvency Ratios Directive.

Opportunities in European Financial Services

I

THE EMERGING SINGLE EUROPEAN MARKET IN FINANCIAL SERVICES

1

The Strategic Challenge in Europe

THE NEED FOR A STRATEGY

As recently as the start of 1989, the strategic questions raised by the European Commission's 1992 program to create a single market embracing the twelve sovereign states that are the European Community (EC) were fairly clear. For financial institutions already operating inside the EC, the fundamental problems revolved around opportunities to increase turnover and to reduce costs by moving to an integrated European operation; for institutions not yet operating inside the EC, the issue was whether a major firm could afford *not* to operate inside the world's largest trading block. Although these questions have not gone away, the democratic revolution in Eastern Europe has changed the situation dramatically. It is now of critical importance that every financial institution that aspires to invest in major growth areas should have a strategy for Europe.

The benefits of the creation of a single market across the European Community have been analyzed extensively. *European Economy,* the quarterly publication of the Office for

Official Publications of the European Communities (No. 35, March 1988), suggested that the medium-term benefits of removing barriers could be: an increase of around 4 1/2 percent in gross domestic product (GDP); a fall of 6 percent in price levels; the creation of 2 million more jobs; and significant improvements in the total budget balance and the trade balance, even with a relatively passive macroeconomic policy. A more expansionist economic stance could lead to a 7 percent increase in GDP.

Even these estimates—which imply significant opportunities for financial services companies—have been challenged as being on the low side. First, a number of economists are now agreed that even the initial progress toward the single market and to economic integration has produced significant benefits. Second, the dynamic effects on innovation and competition may well translate not into a once-for-all gain but into continuing, faster growth as European firms gain in size and resources.

In addition to these substantial gains, the prospects in Eastern Europe need to be considered. Poland, Hungary, Czechoslovakia, and Bulgaria have a total population of 72 million. These nations' populations are well educated, but their economies lack the infrastructure and modern industrial investment of the Organization for Economic Cooperation and Development (OECD) nations. They see themselves as part of Europe and will predominantly look to Western Europe for support and expertise. The financial institutions of Germany, France, Britain, and the rest of the EC will take the major share of the growth.

Providing financial services to the emergent market economies of Eastern Europe is an opportunity that has to be considered by any strategy planner. European institutions that finance that investment will grow in turnover and assets. As increased investment is reflected in increased personal disposable income, the opportunities for selling personal financial services will grow rapidly. Lacking effective domestic financial institutions, these countries will need the provision of a financial infrastructure.

Further east, and presumably still part of Mikhail Gorbachev's homeland, lies European Russia, which shares the economic characteristics of the former satellites to an even greater degree—high levels of technical training coupled with a near total lack of financial and industrial infrastructure.

On top of the opportunities provided to invest in the East, the process of political liberalization has allowed a significant number of younger people to move to Western Europe, especially West Germany. Thus German industry has not only a larger market to supply with investment goods, such as machine tools, but also the workforce to provide these goods. If these new workers, who offset West Germany's demographic deficit in population under 50, support their families back home, the financial benefits should be considered as it is Eastern Europe that receives the hard currency.

To realize the long-term opportunities in Eastern Europe requires an integrated European strategy, perhaps to an even greater extent than realizing opportunities in the European Community itself, as Eastern Europe becomes first associated with, and then part of, the EC. This European strategy will require an understanding of the political as well as the economic context, because all financial institutions must operate in a political environment. While much analysis has been devoted to identifying economically rational policies for Eastern European development, little attention has been paid to the political and other institutions. But these rational policies have to be implemented through the sophisticated political systems of the sovereign national states of Europe, and inevitably the economic program is substantially affected. A central illustration of the impact of established political values is the demand to add a social dimension to the 1992 process. There can be no doubt now that social values too will shape the development of both Eastern and Western Europe.

The revolution in the East is clearly a revolution of the people against a governmental system that lacked legitimacy. Faced with the impossibility of taking Brecht's advice—"the government had better find itself another people"—politburo after politburo has given way to popular pressure. In the East, a people's Europe is being born. And because the movement is a people's movement, we can be certain that those who are emerging as leaders reflect the values of the people they lead.

These leaders articulate the substantial supranational, pan-European element of Eastern European values. This is not surprising. Forty years of communist dictatorship have largely destroyed pre-war nationalist elements, but have inflicted less damage on organizations that could draw strength from outside. Hence the strong position of the churches in Poland, East Germany, and Czechoslovakia and the popularity of the House of Hapsburg in Hungary. As a result, the concept of the state as a social order, not just as referee, is as deeply ingrained in Eastern Europe as it is in the social market economy of West Germany.

The strong and durable symbols of pan-Europeanism in Eastern Europe also provide a stronger bridge to the EC's social dimension. Anglo-Saxons who broke from Rome in the sixteenth century and have never experienced a Christian Democratic party find the importance attached to Catholic practice hard to comprehend, and they underrate the extent to which President Jacques Delors's Catholicism gives him a basis of moral authority that enhances his political position as President of the European Commission. Americans who have had no doubt as to the role of the Presidency for two centuries and Britons who have had no doubt as to their reigning monarchs for three centuries also underrate the symbolic importance attaching to the status of a Cardinal Primate or, in the heart of Europe, to the name of Hapsburg. These powerful forces are in reality allied. A papal letter recently opened with a salutation of Otto von Hapsburg as "Imperial and Royal Highness," a deliberate statement of the status the Vatican accords to the man the Presidents of Austria and Hungary officially regard as a Bavarian Member of the European Parliament.

These powerful forces are pushing Europe into a single political and economic entity with strong social and market dimensions. Remote from day-to-day business issues, they nevertheless shape the political structure in which businesses operate.

To these must be added one other major force: fear of Germany. Although nearly half a century has passed since the entirety of Europe save only Switzerland experienced the brutality of occupation administered by Himmler, families throughout Europe still bear the emotional scars inflicted at that time. To ensure the future safety of France, Jean Monnet devised an approach to the future of Europe that would tie Germany industrially, economically, and ultimately militarily so closely to France and the other states of Europe that general European war would become impossible. Robert Schuman, the great French Foreign Secretary of the 1950s and mayor of Metz, a city for whose possession France paid with her lifeblood, implemented Monnet's ideas and brought into existence the European Communities. With the reunification of Germany now only a question of when, not whether, completing the integration of the European Community is seen by all the continental members of the EC as overriding. This vision of Europe is essentially one that binds people together, and hence again involves a social dimension that financial planners must understand.

These social issues are particularly well understood by the leading banks in Germany and France. The German banks, as the major equity shareholders in German industry, have been accustomed to working inside the framework of codetermination imposed by the German social market model. French banks are well accustomed to operating in the context of the French economic planning system. Almost all banks are accustomed to far closer cooperation with government than British and American banks.

This has had a price, however. The free-market attitude prevailing in London and New York has helped to create a more entrepreneurial institutional framework. The future shape of the successful institution will combine the social responsibility and long-term culture of a continental bank with the market deal-driven culture of the Anglo-Saxon banks—hence, for instance, Deutsche Bank's acquisition of Morgan Grenfell.

MARKET POSITIONING

Any marketing strategy aims toward successful management of and positioning in the marketplace so as to achieve growth of profitable activities. Because markets change, strategies have to be developed constantly. Successful strategic development results from preparedness to meet changed circumstances. In a world with perfect knowledge of the future, the only task required would be good planning. Because the future is largely unknown, strategy must include flexibility and responsiveness as well as anticipation of changes.

In any European strategy, a number of certainties and a number of uncertainties can be identified. The most secure set of data covers population projections, at least of adult populations, up to about 2025. We can project the population of the whole of Europe; we can segment it North and South; but political factors so influence the East–West segmentation that we cannot tell whether West Germany's demographic deficit (the consequences of a falling birth rate) will be corrected by the influx of 25- to 30-year-olds from the East. The more successful the Eastern European economies are, the greater the demographic imbalances will be in Germany—and the larger the productive workforce will be in the East, thus reinforcing success. Analysis of demographic trends will be of critical importance to the retail financial sector. An ageing population will probably buy more savings-type products, a fast growing population needs more credit products, and so on.

FUTURE GROWTH OF EUROPEAN ECONOMIES

There is a reasonable consensus regarding overall economic prospects in Europe. The completion of a single market is expected to accelerate growth rates throughout Europe, and according to Professor Douglas McWilliams, chief economic advisor to the Confederation of British Industry, this has started to happen. As noted above there is some theoretical dispute about whether Europe will have a once-and-for-all jump in output or continuing faster growth arising from integration. As to national growth rates, it is easier to divide the continent North–South than East–West. Southern Europe seems clearly set for faster growth than Northern Europe. But the impact of the changes in Eastern Europe is unclear, and the performance of individual Northern economies is hard to predict. Financial institutions focused in commercial service have considerable problems in predicting areas of growth, and probably need to minimize risk by achieving a portfolio of European business.

Europe is clearly in the process of becoming free of both tariff and nontariff barriers. Tariff barriers within the EC and between the EC and associated states have disappeared. The Eastern European countries, and possibly even the Soviet Union, will become members of the European Free Trade Association (EFTA). Commercial banking and securities products are increasingly being traded freely, and the removal of foreign exchange control by 1992 will complete that process. Examples of businesses that are already fully integrated include money brokering and lead management of securities issues. The barriers to a single market will be largely cultural: Italian and German ways of doing business will vary, for instance.

The legal barriers to trade in retail financial products will largely be eroded by the 1992 process. Some will remain because the European Commission's mechanism to achieve a single market was mutual recognition rather than harmonization. A more serious issue for strategic planning for retail financial institutions in Europe will be the social and cultural differences already being dealt with by many commercial institutions.

Thus, a planner can be reasonably confident about total market size, the relative North–South growth potential, the removal of legal barriers to offering products, and the probability that, while differences between commercial products will be eroded, some scope for niche marketing of retail products will exist.

THE IMPORTANCE OF MONETARY UNION

This admittedly very generalized scenario would enable some quite concrete prescriptions for strategy planning if it were not for the problems of monetary union. As long as there are eleven currencies in the EC, planners face the specter of differential inflation rates and currency movements. Consider a parallel situation in the United States: state-level regulation does not prevent an efficient financial market; independent currencies would.

The EC developed a plan called the Delors report, to move to monetary union (the committee that drew it up was chaired by President Jacques Delors). The Delors plan is seen by those who prepared it as a single prescription for moving toward an interlocking of currencies so rigid that, in the words of European Commissioner Sir Leon Brittan, a British £10 note would carry a statement of its value in ECU.

We will discuss the stages of the Delors proposals later in the book. Their strategic political implications are of consequence here.

There is some disagreement among the heads of government of the Member States about how far to go along the road toward monetary union. Although several have reservations on details, the only person who appears opposed to moving further than a system of re-alignable exchange rate banks is the British Prime Minister. It is important to distinguish between media hype and reality. Margaret Thatcher's style has produced a sharp division in popular responses: her opponents (including, in the eyes of the media, a majority of the British cabinet) regard her conduct as excessively autocratic; her supporters see her as a Churchillian figure, heroically defying European socialism. Economists have inevitably rushed to provide ammunition for the battle, adding much smoke and confusion but little clarity of thought.

This popular representation is too black-and-white. The situation will be resolved by practical experience (which, as shown by the United States, supports development of the present arrangements to full monetary union) and political muscle. The other eleven Member States can move forward on their own by calling an intergovernmental conference and establishing a common monetary system that excludes Britain. Since the British Foreign Secretary has said that Britain will participate in such a conference and since Mrs. Thatcher will soon need support from the City of London to fund an election campaign, it is likely that Britain will move forward toward participation in monetary union. If this does not happen, strategic planners will have to decide whether the advantages London might offer as a location to produce financial services are outweighed by both financial and political risks because other Member States would favor firms located in other European countries. Neither risk would be trivial, if the experience of the motor industry is a guide. In the years of British exclusion from the EEC before 1973, efficient British component manufacturers suffered in the German market, partly because £-denominated prices were subject to serious fluctuation in Deutsche marks (DMS), but also because nationalist prejudice was respectable when directed against nonparticipating Britain.

INDUSTRIAL RESTRUCTURING

Industrial restructuring will produce demand for financial services. Achieving the significant gains anticipated in economic and industrial performance will in itself produce substantial business in the corporate finance sector. For instance the March 1988 issue (No. 35) of *European Economy* identified 25 products in which firms of the *m*inimum *e*fficient *t*echnical *s*ize (mets) exceeded 20 percent of the production of all firms in the United Kingdom; the cost increase imposed by being half the mets exceeded 5 percent. Similar analyses have been carried out for other economies.

In some industries, for example, the automobile industry, the only way to achieve a minimum size is to operate on a pan-European level. In other industries, only European producers can anticipate achieving competitive size in national markets. The products covered include such consumer durables as refrigerators, washing machines, and televisions.

Restructuring is already taking place, through either mergers or joint ventures. All of these reorganizations require considerable input from financial advisors. As the scale and complexity of operations increase, so do the benefits of treasury management and consequently the demand for sophisticated financial services.

FINANCIAL SERVICES RESTRUCTURING

Restructuring of the financial services sector is inevitable. The completion of the EC's internal market, the movement toward a single currency, and the needs and opportunities of Eastern

Europe will combine to compel a restructuring of the sector. The most likely direction of change in the first instance is toward separation of the production and distribution functions, with producers of financial products looking for outlets that can offer local branding. Examples of this approach in manufacturing are General Motors' branding of its cars as Vauxhall or Volkswagen in the UK and as SEAT in Spain. In the financial sector, Deutsche Bank has developed a similar approach, maintaining the national identities of branches it has acquired.

Two factors will drive restructuring of the financial services industry. The first is the need to service an emergent European industrial structure. The second is the scope to increase profits by product development and economies of scale. The expected macroeconomic consequences of the liberalization of financial services give some idea of the scale of the restructuring that is likely to take place (Table 1–1).

Table 1–1
Anticipated Medium-Term Changes Resulting from Completion of the Internal Market

	Program Components	
Areas Affected	*Abolition of Frontier Controls*	*Liberalization of Financial Services*
Relative changes (%):		
GDP	0.4%	1.5%
Consumer prices	–1.0%	–1.4%
GDP price deflation	–0.9%	–1.4%
Absolute changes:		
Employment (× 1000)	215	400
Public sector borrowing requirement as % GDP	0.2%	1.1%
Balance of trade as % GDP	0.2%	0.3%

Source: European Economy, No. 35.

An analysis carried out for the European Commission sought to identify possible impacts on prices of financial products, to provide an indication of the market pressures institutions will be subjected to by the liberalization of financial services (Table 1–2).

The differences in prices vary sharply according to market structures, levels of demand, and cultural differences. For example, life insurance in the UK was 30 percent below the low average (the average of the bottom four prices) of the other countries listed, while UK home insurance prices were 90 percent higher than the low average for such insurance. Italian car insurance is about 150% higher than in the Netherlands and the UK.

Restructuring will be driven by the need to achieve greater market penetration either by reducing the cost of products through economies of scale, or—more realistically, according to economic research—by developing wider product ranges.

Clearly, the removal of barriers will create some opportunities to promote products in countries where regulations currently exclude them. Thus the scope of personal credit may be expanded, for instance, by increased availability of mortgages.

Table 1–2
Possible Impact of 1992 Program on Prices of Financial Products

Country	*Indicative Price Reductions*	*Center of Range*
Spain	16–26%	21
Italy	9–19	14
France	7–17	12
Belgium	6–16	11
Germany	5–15	10
Luxembourg	3–13	8
UK	2–12	7
Netherlands	0–9	4

On the other hand, the apparent advantage of some products, such as the UK's endowment mortgages, which are repaid by life insurance policies, may well be eroded by removal of specific fiscal privileges. To some extent this event is already happening. (An endowment mortgage is now often more expensive than a mortgage repaid by a new savings scheme called Personal Equity Plans (PEPS), owing to UK tax changes.) Nevertheless, the spread of insurance premiums and bank loans among Member States, as shown by European Commission research, is considerable (Table 1–3).

The most likely pattern of development is that Northern European producers of financial services will seek to acquire or, more likely, enter into joint ventures with Southern and Eastern European distributors. The historic strengths and sophistication of the Northern European providers, whose services are based on the stronger economies, have created strong institutions that now face problems of overcapacity and maturing markets. These institutions cannot therefore expect to increase profits in their home economies and will be attracted by the potentially fast growing markets of Southern and Eastern Europe. The pressure from home markets' limitations of

Table 1–3
Economic Dimensions of Financial Services as Percentages of GDP

Country	*Insurance Premiums (Average 1978–1984)*	*Bank Loans Outstanding (1984)*
Belgium	3.9%	142%
France	4.3	93*
Germany	6.6	139
Italy	2.2	96
Netherlands	6.1	130
Spain	2.5	99
UK	8.1	208

* Figure is for 1982.

growth will inevitably be intensified by competition, following the removal of barriers to trade on financial services inside the EC. Financial institutions that seek to grow will be compelled to use positive cash flows to develop new openings.

Entry into the European market presents a major strategy challenge to institutions outside Europe. The easiest move is to acquire a European institution, and acquisition has indeed been taking place. Since the London Stock Exchange granted permission for stock brokerage firms to be sold (previously these firms were partnerships), nearly 70 percent of market capacity has fallen into foreign ownership, much of it North American. Many other institutions, including British insurance companies and building societies, are being actively investigated as potential acquisition targets.

ACQUISITION IN EUROPE

The problem with the easy route is that most of the targets are already operating in mature markets and offer limited opportunity for growth in profits or business. Investigation of performance potential in these sectors reveals that profit growth is being squeezed toward zero, as shown in Figure 1–1. Only by moving to markets that are less competitive and faster growing will high profitability become possible; hence the importance of diversification into Southern or Eastern Europe.

This problem is becoming acute in most major markets. In some markets such as auto insurance (the largest part of Europe's property and liability insurance market), losses persist. Incomers could find that not only was the business they had purchased losing money but also that prospective stock issues were escalating as domestic firms rationalized by merger. A further complication in such areas as merchant banking is the high proportion of corporate assets represented

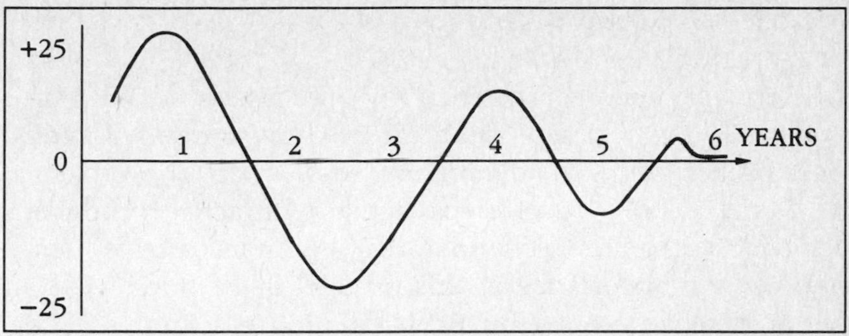

Figure 1–1. Typical annual rate of change in profits as markets mature.

by resource personnel who are able to move elsewhere. Deutsche Bank's acquisition of Morgan Grenfell involved a substantial commitment to the future of the staff, whose departure would have left the purchaser with an empty shell.

This analysis of the problems likely to be encountered in entering the European markets by acquisition suggests that such a policy is rational only when the acquisitor has the strengths to add to the product range or to revamp the management of the distribution process. This requires a careful analysis of changing opportunities and of the strengths and weaknesses of both the acquisition and the target.

Among the issues that firms must consider are further acquisitions—for instance, of a distributor in Southern Europe—or the development of new distribution systems. A direct sales force may be needed, to increase market share in established markets or to develop a capability in new market areas. Another problem an acquirer may need to address is introduction of a new product range to an established customer base. Thus, for instance, sale of equity and other developed savings products may be a feasible option for the acquirer of a savings institution such as a British building society.

BUILDING FROM SCRATCH

An alternative approach to entry by purchase is to build up organically. The Japanese financial institutions have adopted this approach with considerable success. A part of their success is their ability to offer particularly attractive products such as access to the Tokyo bond market. An instructive illustration of the importance of this product is provided by the use of merchant banks by British building societies. The British issuing houses have overall been successful in attracting and retaining building society business in the sterling markets, but the Japanese banks have cornered their Yen business. A potential entrant to the European markets with a distinctive product strength could well consider the route of direct establishment.

DISTINCTIVENESS

Being distinctive is key, and an entrant to the market will have to consider very carefully how to distinguish itself from other firms. This distinctiveness will be needed not only against current competitors but against the financial firm of the future. In particular, the entrant to the European markets (or any established firm that seeks to grow) will have to consider carefully how to position itself against the giant universal banks that will play an important, although not necessarily dominant, role in the future. The most powerful of these banks will be Deutsche Bank. The largest British bank currently is Barclays, which is larger than Deutsche Bank in terms of capital. However, giant universal banks will not necessarily dominate every sphere of activity; the top European lead manager is the British investment bank, S. G. Warburg, a contender that will be hard to catch in this important area.

Choice of a positioning may be complicated by the developments of the 1990s. In recent years, analyses of profitability in the banking sector have suggested that retail banking is far more attractive than commercial banking. This would suggest that entry into retail services might in general be more attractive than entry into commercial services. However, two factors may alter this picture. The first is the growth of competition in maturing retail markets, especially since retail markets are currently far more protected than commercial markets. The second is the need of Eastern Europe for support in developing its financial infrastructure and industrial base. With the opportunities created, commercial banking may well offer increased rewards.

COST REDUCTION

Opening up and exploiting new markets is only part of the strategic challenge of the European economic area. The other part is efficient management of operations.

The key influence in this area will be the 1992 project. As a result of the completion of a single market, firms that currently operate in a number of locations will have the opportunity to concentrate their activities and thus cut back on costs. Apart from the scope afforded by the regulations governing financial institutions, firms will also need to consider the impact of telecommunications deregulation.

As is explained in detail in the main part of the book, the 1992 program is aimed at creating a regime based on mutual recognition rather than harmonization of standards. Opportunities may therefore exist for regulatory arbitrage. To exploit these will require a thorough understanding of the regulatory regime.

THE CONSEQUENCES OF IGNORING EUROPE

Despite the risks and problems involved in entering the European financial markets, the adverse consequences of staying out are potentially considerable. Self-exclusion from Europe would mean exclusion from a developed market of up to 300 million people, and significant weakening of the prospects of serving the needs of Russia. Firms that are able to dominate sectors of the European market will enjoy a base from which to grow into effective global entities. This phenomenon is already noticeable in the most completely international areas, where London-based firms have exploited London's position as the largest international financial center. Firms that exclude themselves from the European market will face competition from European firms seeking a global role. Those firms, however, that seek involvement will require a thorough understanding of the institutions of the European Community, the overall logic and rationale of the Single Market program, and the detailed process of achieving a Europe open for business by 1992.

2

An Overview of 1992 and the Single European Market

The economic movement known as "1992" is not new. From the outset the Treaty of Rome establishing the EEC envisaged the creation of an integrated, internal market that would be free of all obstacles to the movement of persons, services, capital and goods—"the four freedoms," as they are known. The catchphrase 1992, now synonymous with the achievement of a single European market, has come to symbolize the completion of the process begun some 30 years ago.

Progress toward this ideal has been slow, however. Instead of a single, large market open to 320 million people, the European Community is still a series of 12 distinct national markets separated from one another by frontier controls, divergent technical standards, restrictions on the free movement of people, nationalistic purchasing practices, and so forth.

THE UNCOMMON MARKET

Failure to complete the European Community has been costly; according to the European Commission's estimate, the barriers that still fragment the Community cost tens of billions of ECUs every year.

High administrative and transport costs originate from border formalities and their resulting delays. Production that meets the needs of small separate markets with widely differing national standards results in increased manufacturing costs and duplication of research and development efforts. These are only some of what are referred to as "the costs of Non-Europe."

THE CECCHINI REPORT

This study of the costs of Non-Europe, conducted on behalf of the European Commission, attempted to quantify these costs, to identify the many different types of barriers, and to examine the effects on individual industries and sectors. The final report, *Research on the Cost of Non-Europe,* issued in 1988, is an enormous, multivolume document; a brief paperback summary is also available.

Although parts of it have been criticized for making assumptions without detailed investigation, the Cecchini report is a colossal analytical exercise. Paolo Cecchini was appointed as special advisor to the European Commission and was asked to investigate the costs to European business of operating 12 different markets instead of one, within the boundaries of the European Community. Armed with substantial resources, Cecchini brought together a steering group of Commission officials and outside experts and signed substantial research contracts with major consulting and accountancy firms. New methodologies were developed, techniques of integrating divergent data sources were explored, and surveys involving more than 11,000 enterprises were carried through. During 1987, when much of the work was being undertaken, two major conferences brought together the consultants and others participating in the process. The combined executive summaries alone run to nearly 600 pages.

Among the assumptions in the Cecchini studies is the full completion of a single market, up to and including a fully reciprocal Economic and Monetary Union (EMU). Achieving EMU may well be some distance away, however, and integration of the financial services sector in 1988 and 1989 brought banking and the question of reciprocity very much into prominence. We will turn to the questions of reciprocity and EMU in succeeding chapters.

The Cecchini report set out to profile the European Community's home market of the 1990s, the cost of its absence, and the gains that its achievement would represent once the costs of division were converted into the benefits of unity. The advantages will be measured not only in the form of lower prices and costs but also in enhanced social and political structures. Following a brief period of restructuring and adaptation, it is estimated in the Cecchini report, the creation of a single market will add 4 to 7 percent to the European Community's domestic product.

The original Cecchini report's analysis of what 1992 involved was summarized in the shorter paperback version, *The European Challenge—1992,* by Paolo Cecchini (Wildwood House, 1988):

> For all the complexities, the essential mechanism is simple. The starting point of the whole process of economic gain is the removal of non-tariff barriers.
>
> The release of these constraints will trigger a supply-side shock to the Community economy as a whole. The name of the shock is European market integration. Costs will come down. Prices will follow as business, under the pressure of new rivals on previously protected markets, is forced to develop fresh responses to

> a novel and permanently changing situation. . . . The downward pressure on prices will in turn stimulate demand, giving companies the opportunity to increase output, to exploit resources better and to scale them up for European, and global, competition [*page xix*].

The many volumes of the complete Cecchini report provide the detailed analysis intended to support these contentions, but the implications are not limited to the marketplace. The effects of deregulation, or rather the creation of one regulatory zone to replace 12, have implications for the political machinery that will implement the changes and for the liaison between business and those political structures. The Cecchini report uses innovative methodologies to support the predictions for 1992, that a single European market will be a great springboard for Europe's economic emergence in the 1990s.

COMPLETING THE INTERNAL MARKET—THE 1985 WHITE PAPER

In the face of increased competition from Japan, the United States, and the newly industrialized countries, the heads of government of the Member States asked the European Commission in 1985 to put forward concrete proposals to relaunch the original objective of a genuine common market.

The Commission's response was to present to the European Council, in June 1985, the White Paper entitled "Completing the Internal Market." This document outlined a comprehensive and detailed action program for the gradual dismantling of all the barriers that still fragment the countries of the European Community and prevent it from functioning as a single market. It also gave a timetable for the action program to be achieved. The deadline set for its completion was December 31, 1992.

THE SINGLE EUROPEAN ACT

The 1992 deadline has been written into the package of treaty reforms known as the Single European Act (SEA), which came into force on July 1, 1987. The SEA formally commits the European Community to the aim of progressively establishing a single market over a period expiring on December 31, 1992. It defines the single market as:

> an area without internal frontiers in which the free movement of goods, persons, services and capital is ensured. . . .

A further amendment introduced majority voting on most internal market issues, to speed up the decision-making process. Previously, progress would have been impeded by the necessity for a unanimous decision.

REMOVING THE BARRIERS

The White Paper set out a detailed program and timetable of some 300 wide-ranging measures (since reduced to 282) for discussion, adoption, and implementation between 1985 and 1992. These measures are divided into three main categories:

1. Removal of technical barriers. Goals include: harmonization of technical standards for industrial products; expansion of public purchasing; free movement of labor and the professions; liberalization of financial services and transport; and removal of legal, fiscal, and administrative barriers to the operation of business across frontiers.
2. Removal of physical barriers. Key proposals would abolish border controls that presently prevent the free movement of people and goods.

3. Removal of fiscal barriers. The goal is to approximate value-added tax (VAT) rates and excise duties.

The 1992 program is presented as a complete, integrated package of old and new proposals. Some of these proposals were already tabled long before the White Paper itself was produced; others are designed to tighten up measures that have been in force for years.

Removing the Technical Barriers

The free circulation of goods is hindered by many differing national standards and technical regulations. In principle they were designed for the protection of health, safety, and the environment, but, in reality they are frequently used to protect national producers.

The European Commission is approaching the abolition of technical barriers in three ways. First, it is aiming to prevent new technical barriers by requiring that draft standards for products be sent in advance to the Commission so that any potential new barriers can be detected and eliminated.

Second, it has adopted a "new approach to technical harmonization": legislation is limited to setting the essential levels of health and safety rather than attempting, as previously, to reach agreement on the detailed technical specifications of individual products. The precise technical criteria for meeting these essential requirements are to be agreed upon by the various standards bodies and through the European Committee for Standardization (CEN) and the European Committee for Electrotechnical Standardization (CENELEC).

This new approach has been made possible by an important ruling by the European Community's Court of Justice, given in the *Cassis de Dijon* liqueur case in 1979. Under the ruling, any product legally manufactured and marketed in one

Member State must be able to be sold freely in the rest of the Community.

The third strand of the Commission's strategy for the abolition of technical barriers allows for the mutual recognition of certification and testing procedures so as to prevent creation of additional barriers to the free circulation of goods in the European Community.

The proposals that come under this section of the White Paper affect a wide range of products including machine tools, food, toys, construction products, chemical and pharmaceutical products, cars, and tractors.

The establishment of a common market in services, a sector of increasing importance to the economy, is also a crucial element in the 1992 program. Numerous national regulations still hinder the freedom to offer services from one Member State to another. The Commission's liberalization program is directed at both the traditional services (particularly transport, insurance, and banking) and the services related to new technologies in telecommunications, television, and information services.

The liberalization of financial services takes up a particularly large proportion of the total program. The numerous changes proposed across the whole spectrum of banking, insurance, and securities are aimed at allowing consumers access to the full range of insurance, unit trusts, banking, mortgage, and securities products available in all Member States, and enabling financial institutions to offer their services and establish branches anywhere in the European Community, irrespective of where they are based.

At the same time the Commission is proposing extensive liberalization of the movement of capital and of financial transfers and commercial credits. Related measures are being put forward in the fields of taxation and corporate law, which are equally relevant to the financial services industry.

The Commission's internal market program would remove legal, fiscal, and administrative barriers to the operation of business across frontiers through measures such as harmonization of corporate law and taxation, a proposed Community trademark and patent, and legal protection of software and biotechnology inventions.

The available benefits will become effective only if the market remains competitive after integration. Gains will accrue not only from the savings involved in dismantling regulations but most importantly from the dynamic effects generated by the new openness of the market, from the pooling of risk, and from the equalization of interest rates. (See *Research on the Cost of Non-Europe,* Volumes 1 and 9; European Commission, 1988.)

Other key proposals are aimed at opening up public purchasing by improving the transparency of tendering procedures and tightening up enforcement of the rules, to ensure that suppliers throughout the EC are able to compete for contracts on equal terms.

The removal of technical barriers is not confined to goods and services. The free movement of people is also an important aspect of the internal market program, embracing areas such as the right of residence, mutual recognition of professional qualifications and higher education diplomas, and the comparability of vocational training throughout the EC.

Removing the Physical Barriers

To remove physical barriers, the White Paper proposed to discontinue the need for frontier checks and controls on people and goods. These checks currently involve collecting taxes and statistics, screening for banned products, barring entry of diseased plants and animals, enforcing trade quotas, verifying road haulage permits, and so forth.

Proposals covered both the complete removal of these physical barriers and the simplification of border controls in the interim period until they have been abolished: harmonization of plant health and veterinary inspection and certification controls; introduction of common border posts ("banalization"); phaseout of road haulage quotas; and the harmonization of vehicle safety standards.

With a view to allowing the total elimination of police controls on individuals, the program also provides for harmonized rules on the acquisition and possession of arms, drugs legislation, and coordination of national rules on visas and extradition.

Removing the Fiscal Barriers

Among the most controversial of the White Paper's proposals are those to approximate rates of VAT and excise duties. These measures would reduce the current diversity of rates and coverage of VAT and the structure of excise duties, to eliminate the distortions of competition and the artificial price differences among Member States.

THE IMPLICATIONS OF REMOVING THE BARRIERS

To begin a detailed review of financial services without first elaborating on the context would be a mistake. Financial services may well be the least evident area of change for the average European citizen in the 1990s. It may be useful, therefore, to describe briefly some of the key areas where the creation of a single market will be of influence. The following brief description is drawn from the thousands of pages of research undertaken by the Cecchini steering group.

Border-Related Controls

The research analyzed and estimated costs of customs barriers to the trading of goods among members of the European Community. Costs were identified for compliance with customs formalities, government administration of procedures, opportunity cost to the EC, and the economic significance of services in the customs-related sector.

The study was very mindful of the limitations and inherent inaccuracy of some of the previous estimates in this area and concluded that the costs (to firms) of customs procedures were in the region of 7.5 billion ECU for administrative costs and 625 million ECU for delay-related costs.* Administering border control and customs cost governments 750 million ECU; lost trade amounted to about 15 billion ECU. This last huge figure, equivalent to £10 billion, represents an upper limit of 3 percent of trade lost. The lower end of the proposed scale, say, 5 billion ECU, is probably more accurate.

The estimates for this area of study reveal a very important issue that is evident in much of the Cecchini analysis. The research has assumed that the creation of the Single Market will eradicate all border post and customs activity. This, patently, will not be the case. Gathering of trade statistics, and certain police and antiterrorist activities, will continue to be a frontier expenditure for some time. Developments in electronic trade statistics following on from the introduction of the Single Administrative Document (SAD) will greatly reduce some of these costs, but it is unlikely that they can ever be reduced to zero. Thus, if the UK maintains a high level of activity at its borders, but France and Germany release theirs almost entirely (a process which has begun) much of the retained cost will, of course, be concentrated in the UK.

* The ECU, or European Currency Unit, is made up of a basket of weighted currencies of members of the European Community. In January 1990, one ECU = £.74. See Appendix C.

Economic Sectors

Specific economic sectors will be affected to a varying extent. The Commission undertook research in several of them, including foodstuffs. Remarkably, some experts argue that the number of trade barriers to international trade in foodstuffs is growing. Significantly, no EC company has established a truly European place in the market although some outsiders have.

Among the difficulties that must be addressed by the single-market process are laws on beer purity in Germany, pasta purity in Italy, wort excise tax in the beer industry in the UK, label details for Spanish soup, and so on. The effect of these regulations is a tendency to focus on national markets rather than European markets, thus preventing concentration and consolidation of industry and economies of scale. Consumer choice is, of course, also curtailed. Some Member States have gone to considerable lengths to protect their national industries; notable examples are German and Danish beer producers, French soft drink producers, and Italian pasta manufacturers. The potential for Member States' maneuvering to prevent opening up of the market has been great. The Danish government's response to attempts to remove barriers is worth describing:

> In 1977, the Danish government enacted decree 136, which banned the imports of soft drinks in non-refillable containers. Three years later, the European Commission ruled against decree 136—reasoning that it violated article 30 of the Treaty of Rome and the Danish government promptly replaced it with decree 397, which banned the sale of soft drinks and beer in non-refillable bottles, imported or domestic. While on the surface it would appear this does not discriminate against importers, the transportation cost of two-way bottles makes them impractical over about 200 km—a distance easily surpassed when exporting to Denmark from most parts of the EC.
>
> In 1982, the European Commission opened a new case against decree 397, but before it could be referred to the European Court, the Danish government introduced decree 95, which

> modified decree 397 by permitting the sale of non-refillable containers, but only in limited volumes and only if a return and mandatory deposit system on non-refillable was introduced. Decree 95 went into effect in April 1985. This last substitution of one decree for another has succeeded in keeping the case out of court, at least to the date of this writing. [*Research on the Cost of Non-Europe,* Volume 2, pages 420–421; European Commission, 1988.]

To succeed in creating a truly *single* European market, the Commission will be faced with many difficulties of this type. The introduction of majority rather than unanimous voting has the effect of making the EC's decisions easier to reach. To implement the decisions, however, will in some instances require more effective compliance and enforcement regulations.

In the foods sector, the research suggested a net benefit of 500–1,000 million ECU in annual cost savings in the 10 foodstuff areas studied. Interestingly, further analysis suggests that the more advanced brand strength and market penetration of non-EC foodstuff corporations operating within the EC will result in a further enhancement of their market position following the removal of trade and technical barriers.

Pharmaceuticals

The pharmaceuticals industry has a concentrated structure: EC companies take 40 percent of the market and US, Swiss, and Swedish companies supply the bulk of the remainder. The non-EC companies, however, produce drugs in dosage form in the EC Member States. All but the smaller EC countries have some national pharmaceutical production, but apart from the large players the predominant focus is on national markets.

The most important factor governing pricing policies is the extensive involvement of European governments in the provision of health care. Lists of drugs that are eligible or ineligible for state reimbursement are common. Effectively the European Member State government is the primary procurer of drugs, albeit mediated by the doctor and/or hospital dealing directly with the patient.

Researchers for the European Commission's Cecchini Report argued that the effects on prices of government involvement, the problems of testing, and the multiple registration of drugs remain as the serious barriers to and inhibitors of trade.

The direct costs of, say, 40–55 million ECU for multiple registration of a new drug (i.e., application for official sanction to each of the 12 Member States) are not the major problem from a cost point of view. Researchers identify the long delays in securing approval as the real inhibitor to development in the pharmaceuticals sector. The EC average for registration is 18 to 24 months, even though there is an agreement in effect that identifies 120 days as the target. With a nine-year average research and development period to bring a drug to the point of application for registration, the problems in this sector begin to become more apparent. Clearly, directives to simplify the process of registration, preferably on a pan-European basis, are required.

The transparency directive has been welcomed by members of the pharmaceuticals industry, who expect it to weaken pressure from governments to expand their local activities.

Convergence of national price levels within the European Community is widely anticipated, although the continuation of a wide range of costs, forms of government reimbursement, and cultural tradition will certainly slow down this convergence.

The Automobile Industry

The European automobile industry is an excellent example of how technical, physical, and fiscal barriers inhibit trade. The situation of the industry is increasingly complex as major producers respond to the massive Japanese investment currently being made in Europe, especially in the UK. Although it is not appropriate to discuss the sector in detail here, specific factors can be noted under the three major types of barriers to trade.

Technical barriers

- Lack of EC-wide type-approval procedure
- Unique national equipment requirements—dim-dip lights in the UK, yellow headlamps in France, special rear reflectors in Germany

Physical barriers

- Border crossing documentary and inspection requirements
- Customs and immigration checks on personal movement

Fiscal barriers

- Car taxation levels that differ in all Member States
- Aid to "national champion" producers
- Maintenance by some Member States of price regulations

HALFWAY TO 1992

Despite the complexities and difficulties listed above, the process of completing the internal market, set in motion by the White Paper in 1985, is already well underway. In November 1988 the European Commission produced a midterm progress report to mark the halfway point in the Single Market program. This report reiterated the conclusion reached by the European Community heads of state at the June 1988 Hanover Summit: a single market has now "reached the point where it is irreversible."

A fifth progress report by the Commission on the progress made toward completion of the White Paper was produced in March 1990. Of the original 300 or so timetabled measures in the 1985 White Paper, 60 percent have already been adopted or agreed upon. (By the end of February 1990, the Council had adopted or agreed upon 158 measures.) The report states that all the proposals announced in 1985 have now been tabled by the Commission and others have been revised, withdrawn, or superseded. A number of additional proposals have also been put forward, reflecting new priorities (e.g., the "insider trading" directive).

Significant progress has been made in some areas such as public procurement, financial services, and technical standards, but others have fallen behind schedule, as in the controversial areas of animal and plant health, taxation, and frontier controls, where many difficult problems are still far from being resolved.

Financial services is an area of the program where considerable progress has been made. In the banking sector, the landmark Second Banking Coordination Directive has been adopted, together with supporting directives on the solvency ratios, own funds, and annual accounts of banks; in the field of insurance, directives have been adopted on legal expenses insurance, credit insurance, and non-life insurance, and agreement has been reached on life insurance and motor vehicle insurance. Important steps taken in the area of securities are: the adoption of the directives on collective investment undertakings for transferable securities (UCITS), major shareholdings, listing particulars, public offer prospectuses, and insider trading. A directive has also been adopted on liberalizing capital movements associated with securities transactions.

As the above brief résumé illustrates, the 1992 program is extremely wide-ranging and comprehensive. Some proposals are highly specific to particular sectors or industries; others, such as those on taxation and corporate law and on the removal of frontier controls, are more universal in application. Before considering the many internal market proposals that are of particular relevance to the financial services industry, let us turn to the institutional structure of the European Community. Understanding the single-market program and the role of the EC in the current political climate in Europe requires consideration of how the European Community came to be and how it operates.

3

The Structure and Workings of the European Community

THE INSTITUTIONAL STRUCTURE

The integration of the European coal and steel industries through the establishment of the European Coal and Steel Community (ECSC) in 1951 was followed six years later by the signing of two further treaties. In 1957 the Treaty of Rome established the Common Market or European Economic Community, intended to reduce the trade barriers among Member States. In the same year, a treaty created the European Atomic Energy Community (EURATOM), intended to coordinate the development of nuclear power for peaceful purposes and prevent increased disagreement on such a key subject among the signor nations.

What we refer to as the European Community is therefore three Communities:

- The European Economic Community (EEC)
- The European Coal and Steel Community (ECSC)
- The European Atomic Energy Community (EURATOM)

These three Communities share the same institutions and the term "European Community" is commonly used to mean all three together. Following is a brief description of the major Community institutions and the way they work.

The Member States

The European Community (EC) was formed by the three treaties described above and now covers 12 countries. From 1957 to 1971 several attempts to enlarge the Community were made. The United Kingdom was effectively excluded throughout the 1960s by General Charles De Gaulle's veto, but in 1973 the UK, Ireland, and Denmark expanded the original six to nine. Greece joined in 1981, and Spain and Portugal completed the 12 in 1986. Austria has formally filed its application to join (while still intent on maintaining its political neutrality) and Turkey formally applied in 1987.

Since October 1989 the scenarios for an expanded European Community have been many and various. At one level the European Commission, and indeed the entire Community, is prepared to see East Germany become a full member through the process of a German reunification. Chancellor Helmut Kohl has set out a program for a unification process but it is by no means clear that the East Germans relish the prospect of being swallowed whole.

In the meantime, President Jacques Delors has also commented that a 20- or 22-member European Community was conceivable by 2000 A.D. This scenario would almost certainly create a two-tier Community, with the original 12 sharing the institutions, and EFTA and the newly liberalizing East European countries sharing a free trade economic space with the 12. Remarkably, in November 1989 the Soviet Union, which had not recognized the institutions of the European Community in November 1987, signed an agreement with the EC.

The Commission

The Commission of the European Communities is based largely in Brussels but maintains information offices in each of the Member States and delegations in many of the world's capitals.

As a civil service the Commission is very much in the French tradition. Not only can the Commission initiate legislation but it has wide discretion within the limits set by existing legislation and institutions. Some people who are unused to this are often surprised at the openness of Commission officials and their willingness to discuss and interpret. The Commission acts as:

- A policy planning body. The Commission has the exclusive power to initiate Community legislation; it alone can make proposals to the Council of Ministers.
- An executive. It implements Community policy based on decisions of the Council of Ministers and on treaty provisions.
- A watchdog. It is the guardian of the treaties and the "conscience" of the Community. It ensures that Community rules are respected, and can, as a last resort, take governments or firms to the Court of Justice for breaches of Community law.
- A diplomatic service. It can negotiate on behalf of the Community and mediate among governments. The Commission President's role in European summit meetings is on a par with the President or Prime Minister of a Member State.

The Commission is composed of 17 Commissioners—two from each of France, Italy, West Germany, Spain, and the UK, and one from each of the other Member States. Commissioners, appointed by the governments of Member States for four-year terms, are pledged not to seek or accept instructions from national governments or political parties, but to serve the interests of the Community as a whole.

The Commission has its own Secretariat-General and is served by 23 Directorates General (DGs) and several specialized departments dealing with all spheres of life from regional policy to energy. Each Commissioner has responsibility for coordinating work in particular areas of Commission policy but the Commissioners act collectively to take joint responsibility for all actions and proposals (see Appendix B).

The Council of Ministers

The Council of Ministers (commonly called "the Council") is the Community's principal decision-making body (see Figure 3–1). Its main role is to make laws by deciding on proposals submitted to it by the Commission, after consulting with the European Parliament and the Economic and Social Committee.

The Council is composed of Ministers representing each of the 12 national governments. Each country assumes the Presidency of the Council for a six-month period on a rotation basis. Foreign Ministers have responsibility for overall coordination of Community policy, but meetings of Ministers of Agriculture, Finance, Transport, and other units, are held at intervals, depending on the issues under discussion.

The Council is assisted by a Committee of Permanent Representatives (COREPER), which consists of "ambassadors" from each Member State together with their deputies. COREPER prepares and coordinates the work of the Council and assesses Commission proposals before they are considered by the Council at the ministerial level.

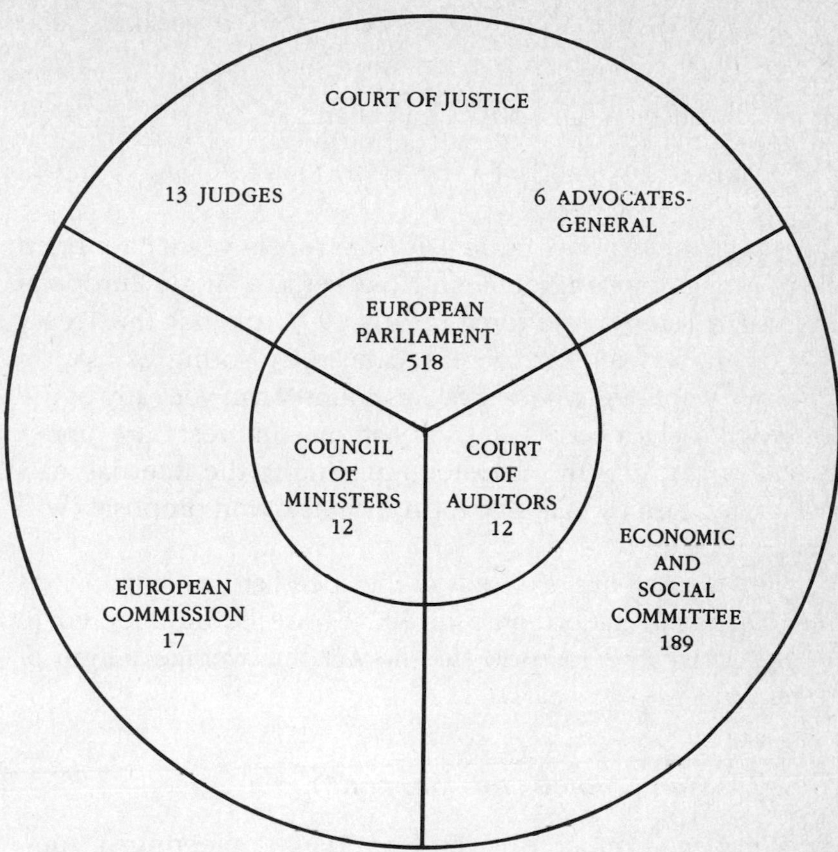

Figure 3–1. The institutions of the European Community.
Source: Spicers Centre for Europe

Council decisions may be reached unanimously or by a simple or qualified majority. For a measure to be adopted by a qualified majority, 54 votes (out of the total of 76) are required.

The votes are apportioned as follows:

10 votes each to France, West Germany, Italy, and the UK

8 votes to Spain

5 votes each to Belgium, Greece, the Netherlands, and Portugal

3 votes each to Denmark and Ireland

2 votes to Luxembourg.

In practice the majority of decisions in recent years have been taken by unanimous agreement. However, the Single European Act, which entered into force in July 1987, amends the Treaty of Rome to provide for increased majority voting except on certain key policies where any one country can veto any of the Commission's proposals if vital national interests are under discussion. Most of the decisions relating to the internal market can be taken by majority voting, but taxation proposals will require unanimity.

This change has accelerated the speed at which decisions are now being made. Some directives are being adopted in under a year, whereas prior to the Act the average length of voting time was two years.

The European Council (the "Summit")

The European Council evolved from regular meetings ("summits") of the heads of government of the Member States and had, until 1986, no legal standing in the Community treaties. The Council meets at least twice a year and brings together the heads of state or heads of government of the Member States (assisted by their Ministers for Foreign Affairs) and the President of the Commission. The Council is chaired by the head of the government or state whose representative holds the office of President of the Council of Ministers. As the final arbiter in negotiations among the Member States, the Council provides an opportunity for leaders to discuss politically difficult or unresolved matters.

The original blueprint for the European Community

envisaged four equally strong partners in the process: the Commission, the Parliament, the Court of Justice, and the Council of Ministers. It is ironical that while the Commission has been the focus of attention and criticism among those of an anti-European persuasion, the Council of Ministers has until recently been untouched. In fact, the Council of Ministers has built up extraordinary powers and it is worth tracing how this power was gathered in by the national governments.

Originally, agreement on proposals was concluded by the "ambassadors" to the European Community—the Committee of Permanent Representatives. Agreements reached by these representatives or their deputies had to be ratified by the minister concerned. If an agreement could not be reached, then a Council was convened on that subject—a Transport Council, Agricultural Council, Environmental Council, and so on. Ministers of state then worked to thrash out the difficulties and reach agreement. The Council itself was, and still is, a Council of Foreign Ministers, who were to meet four times a year and to whom service ministers would pass problems only in the rarest of cases. As Stanley Budd notes in his book, the Council of Foreign Ministers was intended to be "the court of last resort; if Prime Ministers or Presidents came into the act (as of course they often did) it was at the other end of a hotline, through a scrambler usually in the small hours of the morning." (Stanley Budd, *The EEC: A Guide to the Maze,* 2nd ed. London: Kogan Page, 1987, p. 38.)

Through the 1970s European governments were preoccupied with domestic concerns following the oil crisis and the consequent recession. The functioning of COREPER and the Council of Ministers faltered and the European Council, made up of heads of government, took a *de facto* center-stage position. Not until passage of the Single European Act in 1987 did the European Council, as we noted above, have any formal existence.

The introduction of majority voting on many issues and the

slight increase in the European Parliament's powers occasioned by the Single European Act are genuine signs of the times. Effectively, from 1974 until the mid-1980s, individual Member States jealously guarded national interests and went to Brussels to do battle rather than to cooperate. From the early 1980s the return of real economic growth and the expansion of restructured industry and commerce put pressure on governments to redirect themselves to the tasks set out in 1957 and again, with enlargement, in 1973. This process led of course to the Cecchini report, the White Paper, and the Single European Act.

The European Parliament

The European Parliament has a consultative and supervisory role and provides a forum for expression of opinions on any Community matter.

Since the first European elections in 1979, the European Parliament has been composed of members who are elected every five years by direct universal suffrage according to the practice current in each Member State. The European Parliament has 518 members (MEPs) who take their seats in the Parliament according to political conviction rather than nationality.

The Parliament has its administrative base in Luxembourg, holds its plenary sessions in Strasbourg, and caries out most of its committee work in Brussels. The basic work of the Parliament is done through 18 specialized committees that are concerned with particular areas of Community activity ranging from Social Affairs and Employment to Research and Technology. The committees discuss the various legislative proposals put forward by the Commission before they are debated and voted upon by the Parliament sitting in full session. The Parliament then sends its opinions to the Council and the Commission.

The Parliament is unable itself to create or initiate any legislation. It is essentially concerned with influence, because the Commission can take no action without seeking the opinion of Parliament.

However, the Parliament does have some formal powers, including growing powers over the Community budget and the right to dismiss the Commission (over which it exercises general supervision) by a vote of censure. In November 1989 the Parliament threatened to sack the Commission following its revision of the Social Charter proposals in the face of criticism from the United Kingdom.

In addition, the Commission and the Council are answerable to Parliament in that MEPs may question them about any aspect of Community activity. Questions may be in writing or they may be put down for oral reply during a Parliamentary sitting. Questions and answers are published in the *Official Journal* of the European Communities.

The Single European Act amends the Treaty of Rome to allow for more direct involvement in the decision-making process by the European Parliament. Through the introduction of a new cooperation procedure, where a qualified majority of the Council, acting in cooperation with the Parliament, can make certain decisions relating to the internal market, social policy, economic and social cohesion, and research.

The procedure gives the Parliament a second reading of proposals after the Council has reached a "common position" on them and before it adopts its final decision. It also gives the Parliament the power to introduce amendments to proposals which can then only be overruled by a unanimous vote of the Council.

This new power's great significance has only recently been recognized. For the first time the Parliament has the ability to impose its will on the Council. On certain topics the Parliament could, on second reading, require that the Council take certain recommendations on board and incorporate them. If there is one Member State, no matter how small, prepared to endorse these recommendations, then the Council is bound to take the amendments on board, or to let the entire proposal fail. The opportunity for maneuvering is quite considerable.

It is important to note that this is a significant departure from the relatively ineffectual role the European Parliament had held until recently. The Parliament has begun to recognize its potential and to flex its still limited muscles. One important point to watch will be the attempt currently under way to relocate the European Parliament to Brussels. To be more effective and to exert more influence, parliamentarians believe, their current arrangements of shifting constantly between cities are unacceptable. A major center is currently under construction in Brussels which could, coincidentally, accommodate all 518 MEPS and cater for all ancillary functions.

Perhaps the most significant indication of the growing significance of the European Parliament is the equally growing number of lobbyists who represent all interests. Most make their home in Strasbourg, currently the main home of the Parliament.

The European Court of Justice

The Court of Justice, based in Luxembourg, has the task of ensuring that the interpretation and application of Community law is observed. It is the final arbiter on all legal questions under the Community treaties, settles disputes among Member States on Community matters, and judges complaints about the effects of Community legislation.

Cases can be brought before it by the various institutions, by the Member States, or by companies or individuals. The Court's judgments are binding on all courts in all Member States.

The Court, which has its headquarters in Luxembourg, is composed of 13 judges who are assisted by six Advocates-General. All appointments are for six-year renewable terms of office and are nominated by the member governments. The

President of the Court is elected by the judges themselves for a three-year term.

The Economic and Social Committee (ECOSOC)

This advisory body consists of representatives of the various categories of economic and social activity. Its 189 members are appointed for a four-year term by the Council of Ministers from lists supplied by the Member States. Nominees are usually leading figures who have close links with major organizations and are drawn from three groups representing employers, workers, and various interest groups covering such subjects as agriculture, transport, small businesses, the professions, and consumer protection.

ECOSOC carries out its functions both in full session and through several specialist subcommittees and working parties. Commission proposals must usually be referred to it for opinion before the Council of Ministers decides on the adoption of legislation. Its opinions are published in the *Official Journal* of the European Communities.

THE DECISION-MAKING PROCESS

The process of making decisions within this complex institutional framework and with the sometimes opposed views of individual Member States is a difficult one. The Commission does genuinely canvass opinion at an early stage, and concerned parties can adopt entrenched positions from a frequently nationalist perspective. This problem of divided loyalties has led to the need for a greater role of the European Parliament and the declaration of loyalty to the EC by appointed Commissioners.

Generally speaking, the decision-making process involves four stages (see Figure 3–2).

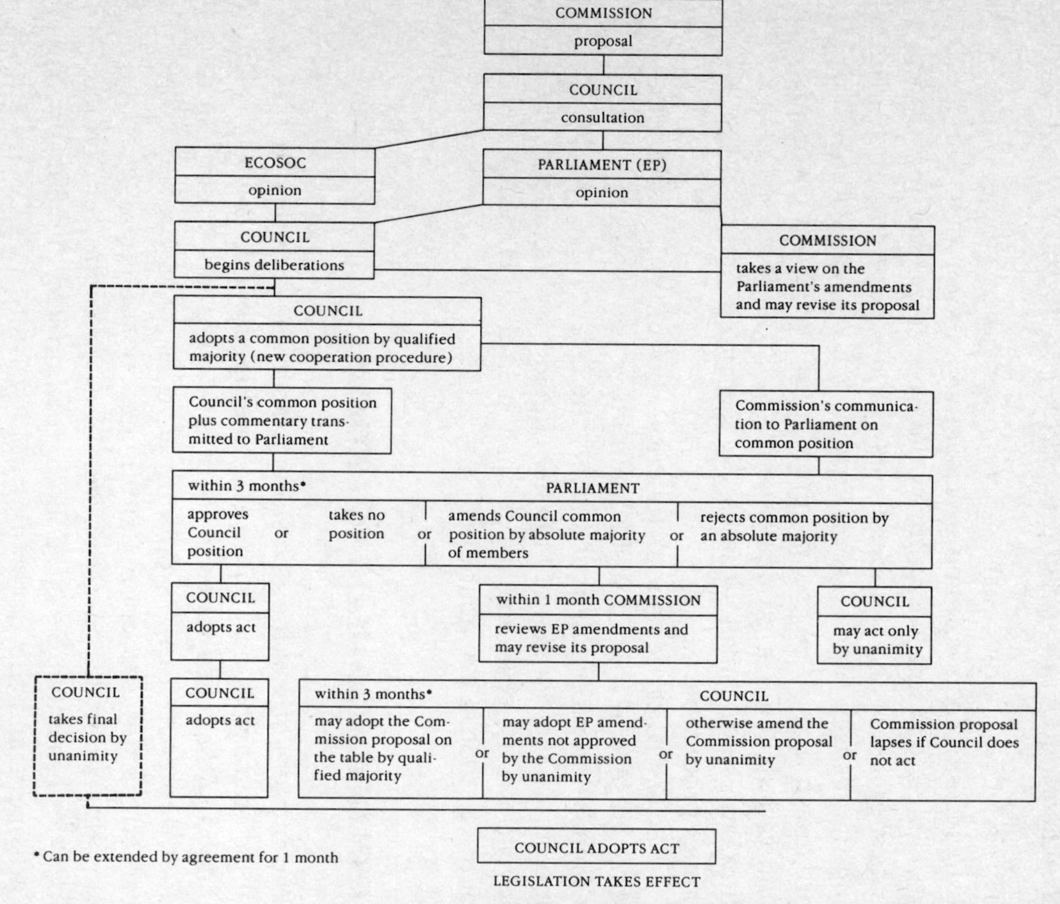

*Can be extended by agreement for 1 month

Figure 3–2. The decision-making process in the European Community.

Source: European Commission

Initiation and Drafting of Proposal

The process of legislation starts with the Commission, which has the power of initiative for all Community measures. Any measure being considered for adoption by the Council must take the form of a formal proposal from the Commission.

In preparing proposals the staff of the appropriate Directorate-General will produce a working paper canvassing the widest possible opinion from member governments, trade associations, employers, and other interest groupings and will be subject to a wide range of formal, informal, political, and technical influences.

Once the first draft has been produced, the consultation process starts. The proposal is passed for discussion to groups of experts from all the Community countries. After such consultations and any further contacts with interested parties, the Commission must formally approve and "adopt" the final draft, which is then submitted to the Council of Ministers for formal consideration and, at the same time, published in the *Official Journal* of the European Communities.

Consultation

Before the Council makes any decision, the proposal is referred for opinion to the European Parliament and the Economic and Social Committee. The Commission is not bound by their opinions, but it may submit a revised proposal in response to any views expressed.

The European Parliament has various specialized committees which examine Commission proposals in detail and prepare reports on them, including possible draft amendments for presentation at their monthly plenary sessions.

The Economic and Social Committee makes a detailed examination of Commission proposals from a technical and professional viewpoint and in so doing consults a wide range of expert advisers.

Consideration by Council

At the same time as the European Parliament and the Economic and Social Committee are preparing their response on a proposal, it is also considered formally by the Member States. The proposal is sent to the Council of Ministers via a Council working group and COREPER where, in the presence of the Commission, national viewpoints are discussed.

If agreement is reached at this official level, the proposal finally comes before the Council of Ministers which may adopt it as drafted, refer it for further consultation, reject it, amend it, or simply take no decision.

Where the cooperation procedure applies, the Council, after obtaining the opinion of Parliament, adopts a "common position" when it reaches agreement on a Commission proposal. This is referred back to the Parliament for a second reading. The Parliament has three months in which to approve it, reject it, or amend it. If the Commission endorses any amendments proposed by the Parliament, the Council may vote by qualified majority; otherwise unanimity is required.

Adoption

Once an item of Community legislation has been agreed to by the Council, it is published in its final form in the *Official Journal* and its implementation then becomes the joint responsibility of the Member States and the Commission.

As a practical illustration of this process, let us trace the progress of the Major Shareholdings Directive through the various stages in the EC's decision-making process.

On December 23, 1985, the European Commission submitted to the Council of Ministers a proposal for a directive on the information to be published when major holdings in the capital of a listed company are acquired or disposed of. This draft directive was also passed to the European Parliament and the Economic and Social Committee for consideration.

The Economic and Social Committee expressed its agreement in principle with the broad lines of the Commission proposal in its opinion given on July 2, 1986.

The European Parliament adopted its opinion after the first reading on April 9, 1987. It approved the aim underlying the proposed directive, but it put forward a number of mainly technical amendments, essentially concerned with improving the wording of the draft.

The Commission agreed to these amendments, and published a revised proposal in August 1987.

The Council of Ministers adopted a common position on July 11, 1988. This contained a number of modifications compared with the original text.

The proposal was then returned to the Parliament for a second reading, which approved the Council's common position on September 28, 1988.

The final version of the directive was adopted on December 12, 1988 and is due to be implemented into national legislation by January 1, 1991.

This means that a full three years elapsed between the Commission's first formal proposal and the final adoption of this directive. For directives, a period of time, in this case two years, is allowed for Member States to implement the directive in the form of national law.

TYPES OF COMMUNITY LEGISLATION

The Community institutions may issue directives, regulations, decisions, and recommendations and opinions (see Figure 3–3).

- *Directives* are binding as regards the results to be achieved, but leave the mode and means to the discretion of the Member States. Directives usually set a time limit for governments to comply.

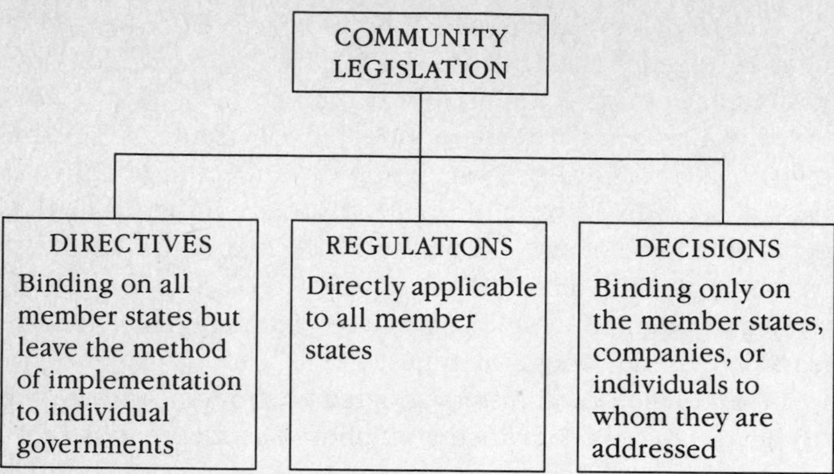

Figure 3–3. Types of EC legislation.
Source: European Commission

- *Regulations* are of general application, binding in every respect, and automatically become part of national law in the Member States.
- *Decisions* relate to individual cases and are binding on the Member States, companies, or individuals to whom they are addressed.
- *Recommendations and opinions* have no legal force but offer guidance to governments.

The enforcement of Community legislation is primarily the responsibility of national governments, but the Commission is empowered to take action against breaches, leading ultimately to a judgment by the European Court of Justice.

This objective description of the European Community's institutional structure gives little indication of how the importance of the Commission has grown. There are several reasons for this. First, the increasing role of the Commission in drafting legislation that eventually becomes a part of the legal framework in each Member State naturally draws attention (and lobbyists) to Brussels from leading corporations in key economic sectors. Second, the expansion of the European Community to 12 Member States has made it more difficult for larger leading economies to direct the development of the Community. Divisions among Member States which involve the Danes, the French, or the British create a context in which the Commission's profile as mediator is raised.

Finally, several key Commissioners have played major roles. Commission President Jacques Delors has displayed remarkable political acumen as his presidency has overseen the emergence of the European Community from relative obscurity to center stage. Several other Commissioners have also demonstrated great ability and independence in steering a course through difficult and uncharted waters, particularly with regard to a single market. Martin Bangemann of West Germany, Frans Andriessen of the Netherlands, Peter Sutherland of Ireland, and Sutherland's successor, Leon Brittan of the UK, have all made a particularly strong contribution to the process of European integration in the economic field and, in particular, to making 1992 the best known (if perhaps least understood) date in the business calendar this century. (The full list of current Commissioners (as of April 1990) can be seen in Appendix B.)

4

1992 and the Financial Services Industry

CREATING A EUROPEAN FINANCIAL AREA

One of the 16 major studies commissioned in the course of preparing the Cecchini report focused on the cost of "Non-Europe" in financial services.

The report covered three primary areas: assessment of the importance of financial services to the European Community's economy; analysis of the present organization of the market for financial services; and evaluation of the economic impact of completing a single market in financial services. The report was based on a study of the financial services sector in all EC Member States except Greece, Ireland, Portugal, and Denmark which, as poorer or smaller economies, have less influence and impact on the development of financial services.

In the financial sector, Cecchini noted that "An order of magnitude of ECU 22 billion is the estimate for the gains forecast by the research for the eight EC countries studied." (Cecchini, *The European Challenge—1992,* page 37; Wildwood House, 1988.)

Current price variations from country to country were analyzed for a selection of financial services ranging from medium-size commercial loans to a mortgage on a domestic property. (See Figure 4–1.)

Substantial price variations clearly exist within the EC; their range is possibly greatest in the insurance field. Most striking of all the statistics, however, are those that show the immense size and significance of the financial services sector.

Table 4–1 shows that employment in the banking, finance, and insurance sectors in the countries studied exceeded 3.1 million in 1985. Banking and finance employed in excess of 1.7 million; and more than 700,000 were employed in insurance. (The figures exclude Italy and Spain, for which there is no breakdown between employment in insurance and banking.) Banking, finance, and insurance represented 3.5 percent of total employees in the eight countries in 1985. Individually, most countries were close to this average except Luxembourg at 7.7 percent and Italy at 2.5 percent.

The financial services sector has become increasingly important to the European economy, and represents nearly 7 percent of the EC's gross domestic product (GDP) ranging from 14 percent in Luxembourg to 4.5 percent in France. As shown in Table 4–1, the financial services sector provides about 3 million jobs or about 3.5 percent of total EC employment.

Financial services are, however, one of the most highly regulated and protected markets in the EC. In several Member States, national rules still contain a body of discriminatory practices and administrative or regulatory obstacles that impede or disrupt the free movement of capital and the free provision of financial services.

The Cecchini report provides further indices of the importance of financial services to the economies of the EC in terms of value added and turnover. "In 1985, value added at market prices in credit and insurance . . . represented 6.7% of GDP. The countries with the highest contribution were Luxembourg

Banking services

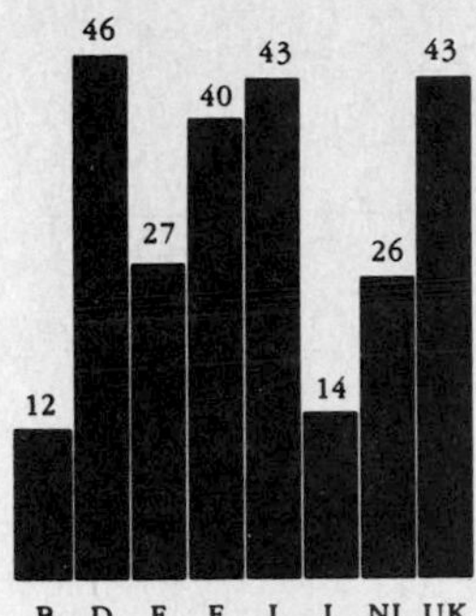

Consumer credit: annual cost of a consumer loan of 500 ECU[1]

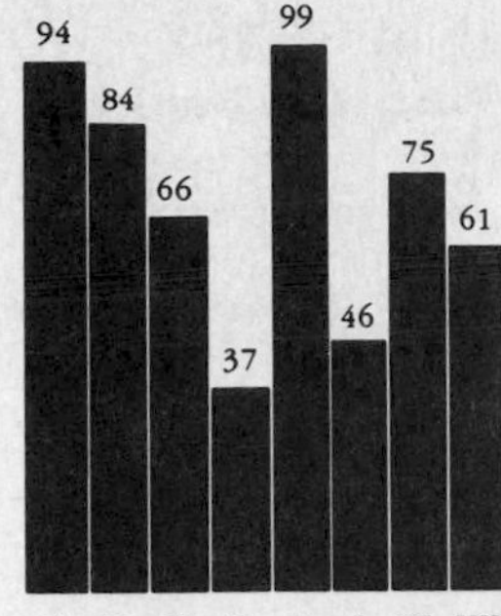

Credit cards: annual cost of 500 ECU debt[1]

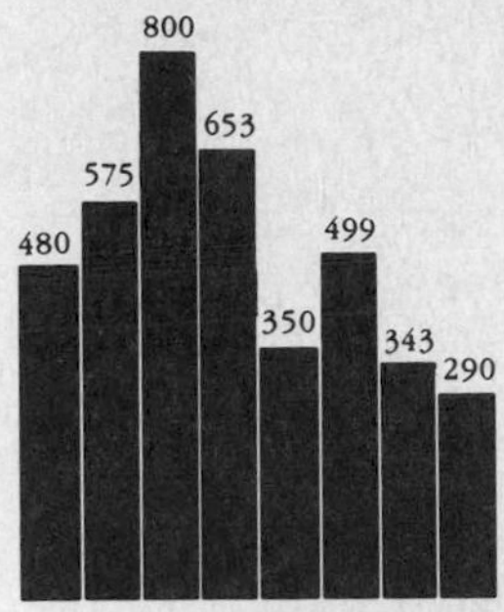

Mortgage: annual cost of a home loan of 25,000 ECU[1]

Insurance services

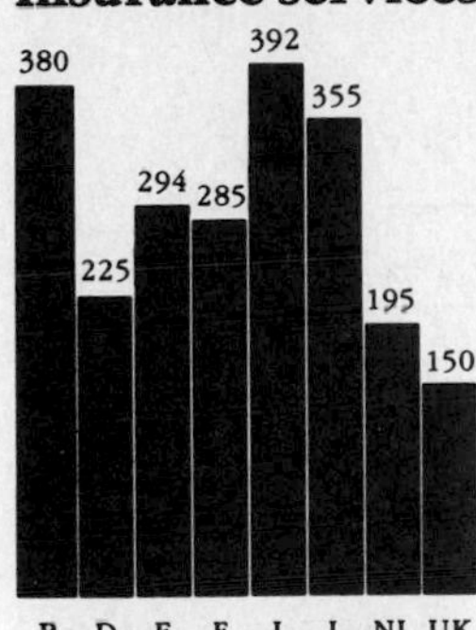

Life insurance: average annual cost of 5- and 10-year term policies for a range of ages

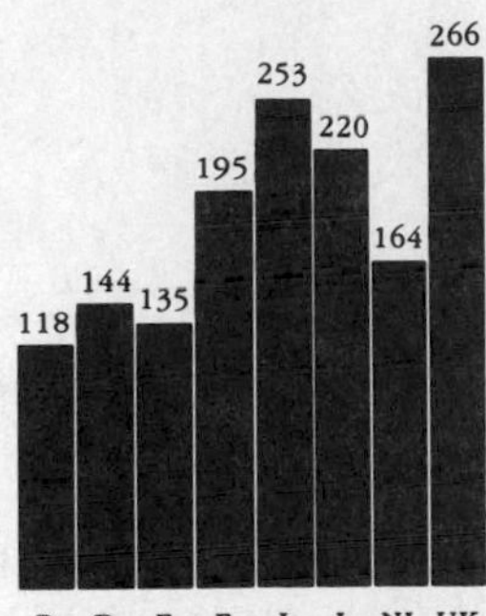

Home insurance: annual cost of fire and theft coverage for home in medium-sized town, valued at 70,000 ECU with 28,000 ECU contents

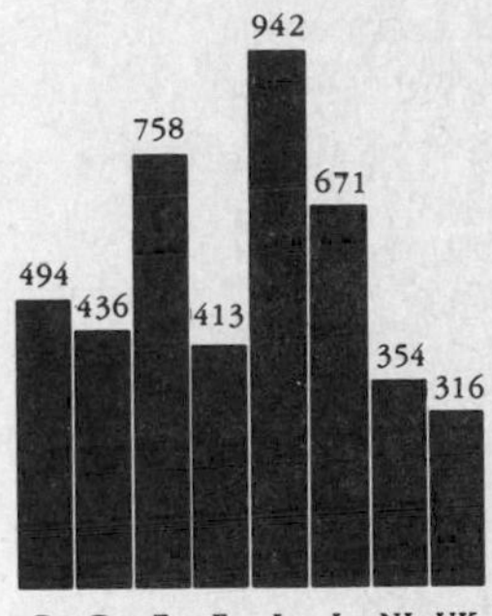

Auto insurance: annual cost of comprehensive insurance for 1.6 liter car—full no-claims bonus

Securities services

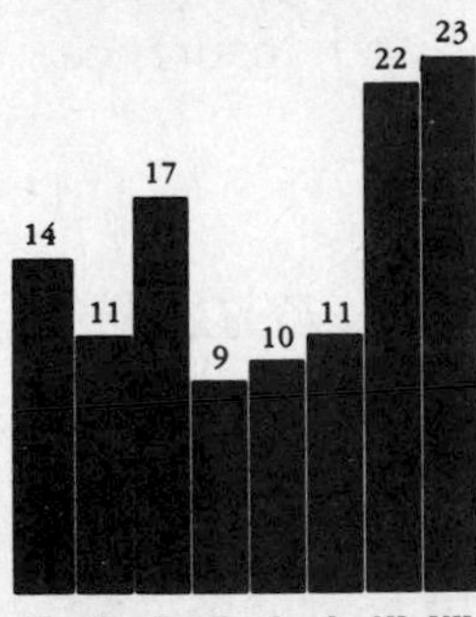

Private equity transaction: commission costs of cash bargain of 1,440 ECU

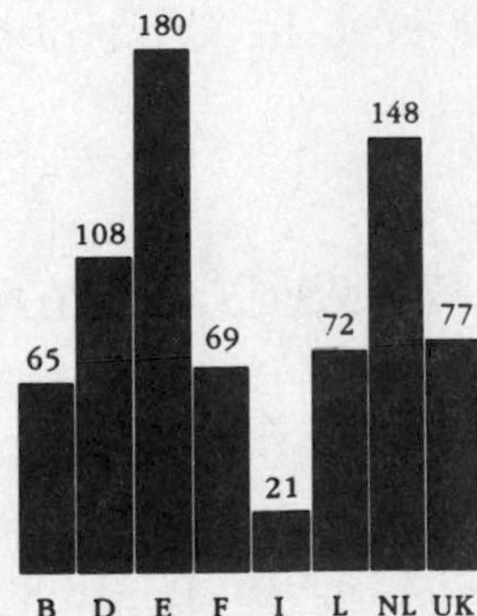

Private gifts transaction: commission costs of cash bargain of 14,000 ECU

Legend

B	Belgium
D	Denmark
E	Spain
F	France
I	Italy
L	Luxembourg
NL	Netherlands
UK	United Kingdom

[1] Difference between interest rates and national money market rates.

Figure 4–1. Comparative prices (ECU) for selected financial services in eight European Community countries.

Source: European Commission

Table 4–1
Employment in Banking and Insurance by Country, 1985

Country	*Employment (000s)*			*Total as Percentage of Total Employees*
	Banking and Finance	*Insurance*	*Total*	
Belgium	89	30.0	119	3.9%
Denmark	604	230	834	3.7
Spain	n.a.	n.a.	292	3.9
France	448	154	602	3.4
Italy	n.a.	n.a.	379	2.5
Luxembourg	9.9	0.9	11	7.7
Netherlands	111	42	153	3.5
United Kingdom	527	245	772	3.6
Total			3,162	3.5%

Source: Statistical Office of the European Commision (SOEC)
Note: These data exclude agents not acting as principals in the financial sector.

(14.0%) and the UK (12.6%). The lowest percentages were in France, Netherlands and Germany." (*Research on the Cost of Non-Europe, Volume 1,* page 269; European Commission, 1988.) The turnover figures further endorse the scale of the sector and again identify Luxembourg and the United Kingdom as the largest in terms of turnover relative to GDP. Banking and securities turnover is largest in Luxembourg and insurance turnover is largest in the UK.

THE MARKET FOR FINANCIAL SERVICES TODAY

The Cecchini report's study of financial services has assessed the current structure of the market. In the area of exchange controls, free movement of capital is allowed in Germany, the Netherlands, Belgium, and Luxembourg; France and Italy are in the process of removing such controls; Spain retains certain controls, as do Portugal and some of the other, poorer economies not studied in the Cecchini analysis. There is no great economic or political significance to the retention of controls in the smaller economies, but exchange controls in the larger economies represent an important barrier to trade and have acted as important bargaining points in the UK–EC debates on joining the European Monetary System's exchange rate mechanism (ERM). Many observers, however, have pointed out that the remaining controls in France, a major feature in the debates on capital movements, are in fact negligible and of little importance.

There is no barrier to the establishment of foreign banks (i.e., non-national banks) within any of the eight EC countries studied by Cecchini. The banks are required, however, to comply with domestic procedures. Control does exist in all countries on the acquisition of domestic banks by foreign operations. These subjects are covered in more detail in Chapter 5, A Common Market in Banking Services.

Some countries require bank branches to maintain minimum endowment capital levels and solvency ratios. The ratios vary from Member State to Member State. Here, observers have identified a clear barrier to trade and a need for agreement or harmonization, and considerable progress has been made by the EC on these matters since the Cecchini report.

Insurance is in a position similar to banking, i.e., there is freedom to establish but only within the context of the host country's regulatory framework. The Cecchini report notes that generally a permanent presence is required in the host country in order to sell insurance, that Member States may insist that insurers have a permanent presence, and that some of the eight countries studied have discriminatory tax measures against foreign insurers.

Trade in securities is often carried out by banks. Consequently the requirements for establishment of banks apply here too. The Cecchini report notes:

> The major obstacle to establishing a presence in a foreign securities market would appear to be regulations which prevent foreigners being licensed as brokers. However, this may not be a significant drawback if securities may be dealt directly between banks. Some difficulties may be encountered for companies which wish to offer only security trading, in markets such as Germany and Belgium, where full banking licenses can only be obtained if a full range of services is offered. There are some signs of an easing in this position though. There are also restrictions on the establishment of offices to solicit secondary market business and on dealing directly with the public to execute such business.[*Research on the Cost of Non-Europe, Volume 1,* page 273; European Commission, 1988.]

LIBERALIZATION OF FINANCIAL RESTRICTIONS

Since completion of the Cecchini report, the European Commission has been active in moving to redress some of the imbalances and barriers to trade mentioned above. Chapter 5, on banking services and 1992, will spell out precisely what these developments and changes have been, but the basic principles behind the 1992 "freeing" of the financial services sector can be noted here.

In its 1985 White Paper (see Chapter 2), the Commission described its approach to the liberalization of the services sector as a process of facilitating the free movement of "financial products"—insurance policies, mortgages, consumer credit, and participation in unit trusts—by using a minimal coordination of rules as the basis of mutual recognition by Member States of what each does to safeguard the interests of the public. The principles and strategies involved are listed in Figure 4–2.

The notion of an integrated European financial area presupposes the creation of a financial free-trade area, where there are no barriers and where no discrimination impedes the free flow of capital and of services. This freedom should be set

The Principles	**The Strategies**
Freedom of Establishment—to set up branches anywhere in the EC	*Minimum harmonization* of national standards for the supervision of financial institutions and for the protection and information of investors.
Freedom of Services—to sell financial services across Community borders	*Mutual recognition* of the way in which each Member State applies these standards.
Freedom of Capital Movements	*Home country control*—supervision of the institution by the authorities of the Member State in which the head office is located.

Figure 4–2. Creating a single market in financial services.
Source: Spicers Centre for Europe

within a harmonized regulatory framework governing prudential and fiscal matters so that the residents of the Member States are afforded a high degree of protection. An effective competitive climate should be ensured and distortions arising from differing tax systems, phased out. To this end the Commission's liberalization program comprises a package of measures to harmonize national prudential rules (in order to ensure the solvency and stability of financial institutions) and rules for the protection and information of savers and investors.

These measures, if fully implemented, are expected to create a range of opportunities—and threats—for financial institutions throughout Europe and to result in:

- An intensification of competition among financial institutions, both geographically and among different financial sectors;

- Reductions in the costs of services and a wider choice for consumers as a result (as estimated in the Cecchini report);
- New opportunities through easier access to previously protected, highly regulated markets;
- Corporate restructuring and formation of pan-European alliances.

Firms and private individuals throughout the EC will have access to the financial systems of the other Member States. Borrowers and savers will be able to choose financial products better suited to their requirements and to obtain more favorable credit terms.

Financial services institutions will be able to offer and promote their services in all the Member States, either by establishing a branch or by providing services on a cross-border basis.

HOME COUNTRY CONTROL

In particular, the European Commission's proposals focus on the coordination of rules concerning: authorization for companies and institutions to operate, financial supervision, and the reorganization or, if necessary, the winding-up of companies or institutions in difficulties.

This process of harmonization is guided by the strategy of home country control: the competent authorities of the home country of a financial institution would be responsible for supervising its operations; the authorities of the host country where the institution is offering its services must communicate all relevant information to the home country authorities. The host state authorities, while not deprived of all power, would thus have a complementary role.

The strategy is intended to limit the harmonization process to the essential rules for the protection of investors, savers, and policyholders so as to allow for the mutual recognition of supervisory and authorization regimes in the Member States. This would enable application of the principles of home country control and the granting of a single authorization valid EC-wide. Financial services firms would thus be able to offer their services anywhere in the EC, subject to a minimum of locally imposed conditions.

The Commission's strategy for achieving unified financial markets is thus based on the following three key elements:

1. Harmonization of the essential standards for prudential supervision and for the protection of investors, depositors, and consumers. This includes the setting of minimum EC standards in such areas as capital adequacy, solvency ratios, monitoring and control of major risks, and guarantees to depositors.

2. Mutual recognition of the way in which each Member State applies those standards.

3. Based on the first two elements, application of the principle of home country control and supervision of financial institutions operating in other Member States.

Banks, building societies, insurance brokers, and any other financial intermediaries authorized to do business in their home Member State would be granted a license, or a single passport, to set up branches anywhere else in the EC or to sell services across EC frontiers.

The position of non-EC banks and financial institutions in this equation has been a vexed question. Finally resolved by the redrafting of the second banking directive, the debate throughout 1988 centered on whether American and other non-EC banks would have equal access to the European markets. The debate raised the question of reciprocity and accusations that the European Commission was seeking to establish a "fortress Europe." We will return to this issue in Chapter 11, which deals with doing business in Europe.

THE WHITE PAPER—A RETROSPECT

The European Commission's proposals for the liberalization of financial services, as outlined in its 1985 White Paper, fell under the three headings of securities, banking, and insurance. Among the prerequisites for creating a single market in financial services were the removal of exchange controls and a curbing of fiscal constraints. However, unless taxation is harmonized, there will be a tendency, for example, for savings to move from high to low tax areas.

The impact on provision of services will not be known until sometime well into the 1990s. Certainly, in writing this book there is no presumption that either wholesale or retail financial services provision will be radically restructured in the short term. There is already a thoroughly international basis to financial services at the wholesale or major-corporation level, but it is by no means certain that customers at the retail level will move significantly to new, non-national service suppliers. Mergers and acquisitions of financial services companies in the middle ranking countries, a process already begun, will probably be the first major consequence.

Nonetheless, the financial services map of Europe is being redrawn and there are major long-term implications. The next several chapters will look in turn at the key components in this reorganization process: banking, insurance, securities, and capital movements.

II

THE PROPOSALS: A CLOSER LOOK

5

A Common Market in Banking Services

The European Commission is actively engaged in a comprehensive program of harmonization measures designed to create a truly internal market in banking. This liberalization process, based on the 1985 White Paper concepts of harmonization of essentials, mutual recognition, and home country control, is also being applied in the insurance and securities sectors.

The foundations of a single banking market have already been laid, with the adoption of EC banking legislation dating back to 1973. The First Banking Coordination Directive 77/780, adopted in 1977, took the first significant steps toward harmonizing conditions for freedom of establishment for banks throughout the European Community. The directive laid down common minimum standards for licensing banks and removed most of the obstacles to EC banks' setting up subsidiaries in other Member States, by banning all discrimination on the grounds of nationality. This means that a bank from another Member State cannot be subjected to more stringent standards than those that are imposed on domestic banks.

A Banking Advisory Committee, made up of high-level banking officials, was charged with monitoring implementation of the directive and advising on the initiation of EC banking legislation.

Another important piece of legislation is the Consolidated Supervision Directive 83/350, adopted in 1983, which obliges Member States' regulatory authorities to supervise banking groups on a consolidated basis.

Some obstacles nevertheless still remain. A bank wishing to set up a branch in another Member State still has to obtain prior authorization from the supervisors in the host country. It remains subject to supervision by the host country and its range of activities may be restricted by host country regulations. Moreover, the freedom to provide banking services across EC borders is not currently possible in all Member States.

The European Commission's proposals are aimed at removing such barriers and allowing banks the freedom to offer services and establish branches wherever they wish in the EC, subject to home country control and supervision. In other words, banks would require authorization to operate EC-wide from only the Member State in which their head office is situated. The proposals would entail mutual recognition, by the supervisory banking authorities in each Member State, of the authorization and supervisory systems in the other Member States.

To allow such mutual recognition and home country control, essential standards of supervision and financial stability first have to be harmonized. To this end a package of complementary proposals has been put forward and a number of directives are now being put in place relating to such matters as own funds, monitoring of large exposures, solvency ratios, accounting requirements, electronic payments, and winding-up.

THE BANK ACCOUNTS DIRECTIVE

Adopted in 1986, ahead of the deadline set in the White Paper, this directive sets out detailed rules harmonizing the format, contents, and layout of the annual accounts of EC banks. The Bank Accounts Directive is due to be implemented into national legislation by January 1, 1991, and banks will have to draw up their accounts in conformity with its rules beginning January 1, 1993.

The purpose of the directive is to ensure that bank accounts are comparable throughout the EC so as to facilitate increased mutual understanding of the financial performance of banks in different Member States. The directive applies to banks rules similar to those laid down in the Fourth and Seventh Company Law Directives for conventional companies, but takes into consideration the particular features of the banking sector. The directive imposes limits on such matters as hidden reserves and foreign currency translation.

The problematic issue of "hidden reserves," which was the subject of much debate when the directive was being drafted, was resolved by a compromise whereby banks are given the option of either using hidden reserves or covering unforeseen risks with a specific "fund for general banking risks." The directive stipulates that the use of hidden reserves should be restricted to cases when it is "required by the prudence dictated by the particular risks associated with banking." The coexistence of these two alternative systems has been criticized on the grounds that some banks could enjoy an unfair competitive advantage by hiding the full extent of their losses.

The Bank Accounts Directive also contains specific rules for foreign currency translation, to cover the large amount of business transacted by banks in different currencies. These rules state that spot conversion rates on the date the balance sheet is drawn up should be used to convert assets and liabilities denominated in foreign currencies.

SECOND BANKING COORDINATION DIRECTIVE

The most fundamental piece of legislation in this area is the Second Banking Coordination Directive, described by the European Commission as the centerpiece of its proposals for opening up the banking sector to a single European market by the end of 1992.

Adopted on December 15, 1989, the directive introduces the concept of a single banking license, granted by the home Member State, which will allow credit institutions, from January 1, 1993, to operate EC-wide without needing to obtain further authorization. Credit institutions, which include banks and building societies, are defined in the First Banking Directive as undertakings whose business is to receive deposits or other repayable funds from the public and to grant credits for its own account.

On receipt of the license, banks will be able not only to offer standard banking services EC-wide, but also to engage in securities trading for their own or the customer's account, as well as participate in share issues, related services, and portfolio management and advice.

Mutual recognition of the single banking license throughout the EC would be assured by harmonizing minimum rules concerning the criteria for granting a license and the subsequent supervision requirements once authorization has been given.

Common rules are therefore laid down concerning the required level of initial capital, supervision of the bank's major shareholders, and limitation of participation in nonfinancial companies. The directive also makes provision for strengthening cooperation among the supervisory authorities in the Member States and the rules on professional secrecy. It contains the following key provisions.

Single License

The core innovation of the directive is the introduction of a single banking license permitting a credit institution to operate throughout the EC. The license will be granted by the banking regulatory authorities in the Member State where a bank has its headquarters and it will enable the bank to operate EC-wide, either through foreign branches or simply by selling banking services across national frontiers without having to request an authorization from the host Member State.

The directive sets out certain minimum conditions relating to such matters as initial capital and the suitability of influential shareholders, and lays down the authorization procedure to be followed so that banks may be licensed to operate throughout the EC.

The benefits of the banking license will also be extended to financial services subsidiaries that are at least 90 percent-owned by an EC credit institution and are included in the consolidated supervision of the parent institution. Once authorized, credit institutions will be able to undertake all the banking activities listed in an annex to the directive, provided that those activities are permitted under the terms of their home country authorization.

The significance of this list is that banks will be able to conduct licensed activities throughout the EC, even in countries where these activities are not permitted to domestic institutions. Another important feature of the list is that it is drawn on the "universal banking" concept and so covers not only the standard traditional banking activities but also all forms of transactions in securities, which are not common activities for banks in some Member States.

The freedom granted by the single banking license applies

Table 5–1
Agreed List of Banking Activities

Deposit-taking and other forms of borrowing

Lending, including consumer credit, mortgage credit, factoring (with or without recourse), and financing of commercial transactions (including forfeiting)

Financial leasing

Money transmission services

Issuing and administering means of payment (credit cards, travelers' checks and bankers' drafts)

Guarantees and commitments

Trading for own account or for account of customers in: money market instruments (checks, bills, CDs, and so on), foreign exchange, financial futures and options, exchange and interest rate instruments, and securities

Participation in share issues and provision of services related to such issues

Advice to undertakings on capital structure, industrial strategy, and related questions and advice; and services relating to mergers and the purchase of undertakings

Money brokering

Portfolio management and advice

Safekeeping and administration of securities

Credit reference services

Safe custody services

to a wide range of activities, as shown in Table 5–1. Provision is made for this list to be updated in order to allow for new developments on financial markets.

Home Country Control

Prudential supervision of banks and their branches throughout the EC will be the responsibility of the banking supervisors in the home country, who will have to ensure that banks have sound administrative and accounting procedures and adequate internal control mechanisms. This principle of home country authorization will determine which activities banks will be allowed to pursue. It also raises particular problems since banks in some EC countries currently have greater freedom than others to engage in a wider range of activities, including securities trading. Banks in some Member States will be faced with the threat of foreign banks' being able to transact business in their home territories that they themselves are denied. West Germany, for instance, has traditionally offered a full range of financial services through a system of universal banks but many other EC countries maintain strict dividing lines between securities business and deposit takings.

Moreover, in countries such as the United Kingdom, authorization and regulation of banking and securities are carried out by separate supervisory bodies. The banking directive specifically excludes securities transactions from the principles of home country supervision. It stipulates that, until further coordination, the host country will be able to take the necessary measures to require foreign bank branches in its territory to make sufficient provision against market risks arising out of securities trading. Home and host country authorities will in the meantime be expected to collaborate closely in the supervision of market risk.

Application Procedure

When a bank wishes to set up a branch in another Member State, it will be required to notify the authorities of its home country, supplying information that includes a description of its intended business operations, the address where the host Member State may obtain relevant documents, and the names of the managers of the branch. If the application is approved, the information will be forwarded to the host Member State authority within three months. The home Member State will have to communicate to the host state details of the amount of the bank's own funds, solvency ratio, and any deposit-guarantee scheme.

A bank wishing to introduce services into another Member State will be obliged to notify the home country authorities of the activities it intends to undertake and, once approved, the host country authorities will be informed within one month.

The directive also contains a clause stipulating that a bank's head office must be situated in the same Member State as its registered office. This is designed to deter banks from opting to register in a Member State where standards are less strict in order to evade a more stringent regulatory regime in the Member State where they intend to carry out their main operations.

Host Country Responsibilities

The directive specifies that, pending further harmonization, the host country will continue to be responsible for supervision of certain aspects of banking activity. In particular, host countries will have the right to control supervision of bank liquidity and implementation of monetary policy.

In addition, host Member States may, for statistical purposes, require all foreign branches in their territory to supply information on their activities at regular intervals, as long as the information requested is the same as that required of domestic branches.

Host country authorities also retain the right to carry out on-the-spot verification of information on the management and ownership of a branch authorized in another Member State. Home country authorities will, however, likewise be entitled to carry out spot checks after having first informed the host Member State.

Provision is made for an enforcement mechanism where a credit institution that has a branch or is supplying services in another Member State breaches legal provisions that are in force in the host state and are justified on the grounds of protecting the "general good." The host country can, through the home country authorities, request the credit institution to rectify the situation. Only in emergencies can the host state take immediate action directly against the institution concerned, in order to protect the interests of depositors, investors, and other parties.

Professional Secrecy

Professional secrecy rules stipulate to what extent and in which circumstances the banking supervisory authorities may be permitted to divulge information passed to them by credit institutions. Employees of the supervisory authorities, as well as auditors or experts acting on their behalf, are bound not to divulge any confidential information received in the course of their duties. In certain cases, specific information could be forwarded to authorized inspectors from government departments responsible for the supervision of financial institutions and insurance companies. The supervisory authorities of different Member States will also be allowed to exchange necessary information, but recipients will still be bound by the same professional secrecy rules. A further provision allows Member States to conclude cooperation agreements with third-country authorities on exchanging information, providing the information is subject to equivalent guarantees of professional secrecy.

These rules on information exchange aroused considerable opposition from some countries, including Germany, France, and Italy, who are unhappy about the possibility of information provided to the banking supervisory authority being transferred to other parts of a Member State's administration.

Limits on Bank Participation in the Commercial Sector

The directive sets limits on a bank's shareholdings or participation in nonfinancial companies. A bank will not be allowed to invest more than 15 percent of its own funds in any undertaking that is neither a credit institution nor a financial institution. The overall maximum limit for investment is 60 percent of capital. These thresholds were raised from earlier percentages in response to fierce opposition from Germany, which is concerned about the impact the limits will have on its industry, which is strongly supported by participation of this type.

The reasoning behind imposing such limits centers on the need to enable banking supervisory authorities to make a reliable assessment of a bank's solvency and stability before and after granting authorization.

Reciprocity

Probably the most contentious element of the directive is the special "reciprocity clause" applying to banks from non-EC countries. When the directive takes effect in 1993, non-EC banking subsidiaries will have access to the whole EC banking market when they are approved in just one Member State. However, EC banks seeking access to third-country markets will not enjoy the same benefits. With this in mind, the European Commission introduced provisions aimed at ensuring reciprocal access for EC banks to third countries from which banks are seeking entry to the EC market.

These provisions will have important implications for the way in which EC banks gain access to third-country markets. Reciprocal arrangements between Member States and third countries have until now been negotiated on an individual basis. The United Kingdom in particular has succeeded in securing favorable conditions for its banks in non-EC countries. The preamble to the directive states that authorizations granted to banks will have EC-wide, not merely nationwide, application; existing reciprocity clauses will no longer be effective.

The rationale behind the introduction of the reciprocity clause, in the words of the directive, is

> . . . not to close the Community's financial markets but rather, as the Community intends to keep its financial markets open to the rest of the world, to improve the liberalization of the global financial markets in other third countries . . . and, as a last resort, for the possibility of taking measures involving the suspension of new applications for authorization or the restriction of new authorizations.

It was initially proposed that the granting of an EC license to a bank from outside the EC should be made conditional on reciprocal rights being offered by the outside country to banks from all the EC countries. Every time a request for authorization was received from a third-country bank to operate in a particular Member State, the European Commission would have had to verify that the country in question ensured "reciprocal treatment" for EC banks. The granting of new banking licenses to third-country banks would have been automatically suspended until the Commission had guarantees that similar freedoms were offered to all EC banks.

A great deal of controversy surrounded this reciprocity test, which fueled the debate as to whether a "fortress Europe" was in the making. The test was strongly attacked both by EC members such as the UK, which is host to a large number of foreign banks, and banks abroad, particularly in the US, which feared they might be excluded from the EC because of restrictive US banking laws.

Opponents criticized the ambiguity of the term "reciprocal treatment" and pointed out that the prospect of lengthy delays in obtaining authorization as a result of the prolonged investigative procedure could dissuade non-EC banks from setting up in Member States.

In the wake of such fierce opposition, the European Commission revised the reciprocity provisions. These clarify the meaning of reciprocity and introduce a simplified procedure for guaranteeing access to third-country markets by EC banks, which will avoid unnecessary delays in the granting of banking licenses.

Member States will still have to notify the European Commission when they receive a request to authorize a subsidiary from outside the EC. However, instead of automatically suspending applications pending Commission investigations on a case-by-case basis, the Commission will assess how accessible third countries are for EC banks in a report to be produced six months before implementation of the directive. The report will examine the treatment accorded to EC banks and any difficulties they are experiencing in establishing themselves or carrying out banking activities in the countries concerned.

Where EC banks are found not to enjoy "national treatment" and the same competitive opportunities as local banks in the third country concerned, the Commission may take retaliatory measures, such as suspending or delaying decisions regarding requests for authorization. Such measures will not be allowed to exceed three months and the Council will be able to decide, before the three-month period is up, whether they should be continued.

Where "equivalent treatment" is not granted—in other words, where the third country is not granting the EC banks "effective market access" and competitive opportunities comparable to those accorded by the EC to banks of that third country—the Commission may propose opening negotiations with the country concerned. This would apply where a country's banking laws do not actually discriminate against EC banks but allow more limited freedom than that enjoyed by third-country banks in the EC.

The Commission will forward proposals to the Council, seeking a mandate to negotiate comparable competitive opportunities and thus aiming to secure the same freedoms for EC banks in third countries as third-country banks enjoy in the EC.

This compromise appears to have resolved a highly controversial issue, and probably establishes a precedent for reciprocity proposals in the insurance and securities sectors. The reciprocity procedure will not, however, apply to banks already operating in the EC before the directive comes into effect. Third-country banks established in any EC country are considered as EC institutions and so non-EC banking subsidiaries established prior to that date will be able to enjoy the advantages provided by the single banking license.

It should be noted, however, that the reciprocity arrangements described above apply only to subsidiaries and not to branches of non-EC banks. The directive specifically states that third-country branches will not enjoy the same EC-wide freedoms to provide cross-border services or to establish branches in other Member States. Under EC law a bank must be "established" in order to be eligible for the single license. This important question is returned to in Chapter 7's discussion of the proposed Investment Services Directive.

Committee Procedure

Another area of controversy is the question of which institution should be responsible for making future technical modifications to the directive and the extent of the powers to be accorded to the European Commission in this area.

A compromise was reached over the procedure to be followed to oversee the supervision of the directive and any future updating in areas such as extending the list of activities covered or clarifying terminology used. The European Commission will be able to make any necessary technical adaptations of this kind after first consulting and obtaining the agreement of the Banking Advisory Committee. When the Committee disagrees, the Commission will have to submit a proposal to the Council, which will take a decision by qualified majority. The dispute over "comitology" has also arisen in other areas of banking legislation, notably the solvency ratio and own funds directives. There have been indications that the

Commission is working on a separate proposal to deal with this dispute.

Capital Requirements

To qualify for a banking license, banks will have to have minimum initial capital of 5 million ECU. Special provision, however, is made for small banks with not less than 1 million ECU of capital when the directive comes into force.

Suitability of Shareholders

The ownership and control of banks by non-banking interests is an area of concern because of highly complex banking group structures and the risks of conflicts of interest. The directive thus includes provisions to enable banking authorities to assess the suitability of major shareholders. Before authorization is granted, banks must inform the supervisory authorities of the names of shareholders who possess influential shareholdings in a bank and the sizes of their holdings. A "qualifying holding" is defined as a holding, direct or indirect, in an undertaking which represents 10 percent or more of the capital or of the voting rights or which enables the exercise of significant influence over an undertaking. Banks will also be required to inform the authorities if they become aware of any acquisitions or disposals of holdings in their capital, above or below certain thresholds.

Shareholders will also be required to notify the authorities if they are contemplating acquisitions or disposals of large shareholdings or planning increases or reductions in shareholdings that exceed or fall below 20, 33, or 50 percent. This requirement will also apply where significant changes result in the bank's becoming or ceasing to be a subsidiary.

An obligation to take appropriate corrective action will be placed on the authorities notified, if they are not satisfied as to the suitability of the shareholders or consider their influence to be detrimental to the management of the bank.

The mutual recognition of licenses and supervisory systems and the application of the principle of home country control are, however, dependent on the simultaneous implementation of a number of other technical directives and recommendations aimed at harmonizing the rules on minimum capital requirements, large exposures, and deposit guarantees.

The Second Banking Coordination Directive, which represents a fundamental step toward the completion of an EC-wide market in financial services, will be able to take effect only when the two key directives on own funds and solvency ratios have both been implemented.

OWN FUNDS DIRECTIVE

This directive, adopted on April 17, 1989, establishes a common definition of own funds, essentially a bank's capital base. The European Commission believes that, in order to avoid distortions in competition between credit institutions in a single banking market, rules for own funds must be equivalent throughout the EC. These common standards are initially defined in broad terms, in order to encompass all the elements comprising own funds in the different Member States.

The directive provides a very precise definition of the various constituent items that may comprise own funds, and distinguishes between original own funds and additional own funds. It specifies the relationships among these various components and states that the amount of additional funds must not exceed the original own funds.

Funds for general banking risks are included provisionally in own funds without limit, but the Commission is due to submit a proposal on its final treatment within six months of implementation of the directive.

Provision is made for a flexible review and updating procedure to take account of developments in the financial markets. The aim in the long term is to achieve greater convergence toward a common definition of own funds. A more harmonized definition of own funds is due to be considered by the Council within five years of the directive's adoption.

Member States are to comply with the directive by January 1, 1993 or no later than the entry into force of the Solvency Ratios Directive.

SOLVENCY RATIOS DIRECTIVE

The Own Funds Directive provides the basic figure that is to be used in the calculation of the Solvency Ratios Directive, adopted on December 18, 1989. Aimed at achieving a uniform method of assessing a bank's ability to absorb losses incurred by customers' default on loan repayments, the Solvency Ratios Directive establishes the rules for the calculation a supervisory authority will use in deciding whether to grant a credit institution the single banking license and sets a minimum solvency ratio of 8 percent. In many respects the directive resembles the July 1988 Basel Convergence Agreement on international capital adequacy levels.

At present only eight Member States apply a solvency ratio, ranging from 5 to 8 percent. The purposes of the directive are to standardize and to raise average solvency standards in the EC and thus prevent potential distortions of competition among credit institutions in a common banking market.

Member States are to comply with the directive by the beginning of 1991, but a transitional period will be allowed, during which credit institutions will not be permitted to let their ratios fall. After January 1, 1993, credit institutions will have to ensure that their own funds (as calculated under the Own Funds Directive) equal at least 8 percent of risk assets.

The solvency ratio will be calculated by expressing a bank's own funds as a proportion of its total risk-adjusted assets and off-balance sheet items. Risk-adjusted asset values will be obtained by multiplying the value of each off-balance sheet item by the appropriate risk weight.

Included in off-balance sheet items are activities such as futures trading, debt swaps, currency options, and underwriting of deals on Euro-securities markets. These are listed in an appendix to the directive, which sets out the methods from which banks may choose to measure the risks associated with such transactions.

The Commission is working on proposals to further harmonize supervisory rules relating to interest rates, foreign exchange, and other market risks arising out of open positions taken by banks on securities markets. The directive lists assets and off-balance sheet items in various categories that reflect the different degrees of credit risk they represent. The 0 percent risk weighting, for instance, includes asset items representing claims on domestic governments and central banks. The 50 percent weighting allocated to individual mortgages for residential property provoked a heated debate and exceptions were granted to Germany, Denmark, and Greece. Until January 1, 1996, they are allowed to extend the 50 percent weighting for residential property mortgages to include offices or multipurpose commercial premises as well.

The UK's discount houses are also exempted because of the special nature of their business, which involves heavy position-taking in the money markets.

RECOMMENDATION ON "LARGE EXPOSURES"

Another essential prerequisite for a single banking licensing system is the recommendation, adopted in December 1986, on large exposures. This recommendation is intended to discourage an excessive concentration of exposure to any one client or group of connected clients. Monitoring and control guidelines are laid down for large exposures: a limit of 40 percent of own funds is imposed on facilities granted to a single client or client group, and the total limit on combined large exposures is 800 percent of own funds. These limits may be exceeded only in exceptional circumstances, in which case the supervisory authorities would have to oblige the credit institution either to increase the amount of own funds or to take other appropriate action to rectify the situation. The Commission is currently drafting a proposal to upgrade the recommendation to a directive, expected to be put forward in April 1990. The aim is for the directive to take effect at the beginning of 1993.

RECOMMENDATION ON DEPOSIT GUARANTEE SCHEMES

A further recommendation, adopted in 1986, aims to protect depositors by requiring Member States to introduce, by January 1, 1990, deposit guarantee schemes where none already exists to provide compensation for depositors in the event of the failure of a bank, and setting out certain conditions to be fulfilled by all schemes, existing or planned.

PROPOSED DIRECTIVE ON THE WINDING-UP OF CREDIT INSTITUTIONS

The winding-up directive is concerned with the requirements for the compulsory winding-up and reorganization of credit institutions. It provides for the coordination of activities of supervisory authorities in the different Member States and ensures the flow of essential information among them. As with other financial services proposals, the directive would be based on the principles of home country control and mutual recognition of supervisory authorities. Primary responsibility for the reorganization and winding-up of banks in financial difficulties would thus rest with the home country authorities.

The proposed directive also includes provisions that make host countries responsible for branches of non-EC banks. A license withdrawn from a third-country bank in one Member State could lead to the withdrawal of the license for the whole of the EC.

An amended proposal, put forward in January 1988 and modeled on the Protocol annexed to the draft European Bankruptcy Convention, added a detailed list of the winding-up procedures applicable to credit institutions in the EC. Another amendment defines what is meant in the directive by a deposit guarantee scheme. The directive envisages that deposit guarantee schemes should be introduced in all Member States by 1990 and should eventually cover all EC banks and branches. (A parallel directive proposed for insurance companies is described in more detail in the following chapter.)

PROPOSED DIRECTIVE ON MORTGAGE CREDIT SERVICES

This draft directive, first published in 1985 and later revised in May 1987, aims to liberalize mortgage credit services based on the mutual recognition of financial techniques. Discussions have been halted on the proposal since it has now largely been overtaken by the Second Banking Directive. Mortgage credit institutions authorized in their home Member State will be permitted to offer their services throughout the EC without requiring additional authorization. The directive does not attempt to harmonize national mortgage systems, but instead introduces mutual recognition of financial techniques that will allow them to offer the same form of mortgage credit as they offer in their home country. The aim is thus to promote a genuine EC-wide market in mortgage credit.

The proposed directive will apply to all credit institutions active in the field of mortgage credit, not just specialized mortgage credit institutions.

A credit institution will be authorized by its home country supervisor to undertake mortgage credit activities in any other Member State, in respect of real property situated anywhere in the EC. The home country will not be allowed to impose any restrictions on the use in the host country of financial techniques that are permitted for mortgage credit activities by the law of the home country.

If adopted, the directive will prohibit any discriminatory or restrictive treatment based on either nationality or the argument that a credit institution is not established in the Member State where the services are provided. Any legal or administrative barriers preventing a credit institution from another EC country from carrying out authorized mortgage credit activities in the host state will thus have to be removed.

A credit institution wishing to exercise the freedom to supply mortgage services in another Member Sate for the first time will have to notify the home supervisory authorities of its intentions and furnish certain prescribed information. This would include details of the types of business it intends to carry out, the Member State to which it intends to supply these services, the conditions under which funds will be received and loans granted, and an address in the host Member State.

Unless the supervisory authority of the home Member State has reason to doubt the financial soundness of the credit institution, it will have to pass this information to the supervisory authority of the host Member State within three months of receiving this notification. Refusal to send the information will, in effect, suspend the right of the institution to supply mortgage credit services to the destination Member State.

Mortgage lenders will be regulated by the statutory authority in their home country, which will be responsible for ensuring the financial soundness of mortgage credit institutions.

Monitoring of their activities in the host country will be carried out by the host country's authorities, in accordance with the host country's laws. Any relevant information will be passed on to the home country authorities.

For a maximum period of seven years after the adoption of the directive, the host Member State will also be able to require that both funding and lending transactions be in its own currency, or, where it allows transactions to be in another national currency, that assets and liabilities in each national currency be matched. The institution concerned would, however, always be able to use the ECU as an alternative.

During the seven-year period, Member States will be allowed to limit the supply of mortgage credit from a domestic credit institution to other Member States. This limitation is set at 25 percent of the total domestic mortgage lending of the credit institution in the previous year.

The need for a separate directive dealing specifically with nonbank mortgage institutions has been questioned, since the Second Banking Directive already covers mortgage credit in the list of activities subject to mutual recognition. UK building societies, however, are concerned that domestic legislation will considerably restrict their freedom to operate EC-wide and are pressing for the European Commission to resume work on the mortgage services proposal. Although the proposal has not been officially withdrawn, it appears likely that the European Commission will monitor progress under the Banking Directive and will take specific action against any barriers erected against building societies.

CONSUMER CREDIT DIRECTIVE

The opening up of the financial services market means that consumers will have greater opportunities to open bank accounts in other EC countries and carry out cross-border transactions. The

European Commission considers that, in the interests of consumer protection, a uniform method for comparing offers of credit among EC countries should be established.

A first step in this direction was taken in December 1986 with the adoption of a directive on consumer credit which made it compulsory for banks and other lenders to state the annual percentage rate (APR) of charge for credit, and which anticipated the introduction of an EC-wide method of calculation. This first consumer credit directive, due to be transposed into EC law by the start of 1990, introduced common rules on credit information, advertising, the content of credit agreements, and the relationship between borrowers and creditors.

A second directive amending the 1986 directive was adopted on February 22, 1990. It increases the information that must be communicated to borrowers in the written contract and aims to allow consumers to make direct comparisons between competing offers of credit.

Amendments included the introduction of the actuarial method of calculating the APR throughout the EC after December 31, 1992. Two further annexes added to the directive have set out the standard mathematical formula to be used in the calculation, together with a simple illustration and further examples of calculations.

According to the draft directive, the APR is defined as:

> the total cost of the credit to the consumer, expressed as an annual percentage of the amount of the credit granted and calculated in accordance with . . . (the Directive)

This definition establishes the principle that, for the purpose of calculating the APR, the total cost of the credit to the consumer should be determined by including every item of cost—interest rates and all other charges borne by the consumer—which the consumer must pay as a condition of obtaining the credit.

However, a list of certain items that may be excluded is also set out, including:

- Charges payable by the consumer for failing to comply with obligations under the credit agreement
- Charges payable by the consumer for services or benefits (such as a subscription for membership of a club, association, or cooperative)
- Insurance premiums or guarantees for securing payment
- Money transfer and bank charges

The introduction of a standard method of calculation will make it easier for borrowers to compare the cost of different credit offers among EC countries, instead of having to compare interest rates calculated accorded to different methods that give divergent results.

Currently most Member States already use the "present value" method proposed by the Commission. However, French and German banks will have to make significant changes since these two countries use simpler but less accurate methods than the one outlined in the directive. In Germany the APR is calculated on the basis of a 360-day formula, whereas France uses the proportional method, based on a monthly actuarial rate multiplied by 12.

As a result of these different systems, German lenders are placed at a disadvantage compared with lenders elsewhere in the EC, and French lenders have an unfair advantage because they can quote rates that appear more favorable. The directive is designed to iron out these discrepancies with a view to eliminating such distortions of competition and ensuring equivalent levels of consumer protection throughout the EC. Member States will, however, be free to introduce tougher standards of protection than provided for in the directive.

The directive was fiercely contested by France and Germany but a compromise was reached under which France and Germany will have a transitional period to adapt; they will be allowed to continue to use different formulas for calculating the cost of consumer credit until December 31, 1995. The other Member States, meanwhile, will maintain their actuarial rate and, after December 31, 1992, will no longer be able to change to an alternative method of calculating APR. Six months before expiration of the transition period, the European Commission is to submit a proposal that will allow a single formula to be applied in all 12 EC countries.

BRANCHES OF BANKS DIRECTIVE

Adopted on February 13, 1989, this directive is aimed at reducing the accounts disclosure requirements and thus easing the administrative burden for branches of banks in other EC countries. This would affect the majority of the Member States since, with the exception of Ireland and the United Kingdom, all currently require separate accounts to be published by branches of foreign banks.

The directive is due to be implemented into national legislation by January 1, 1991, and its rules are to be applied to annual accounts for the financial year beginning January 1, 1993.

Once the directive comes into effect, branches of banks established in other EC countries will be able simply to publish the accounts drawn up by their head office. However, certain additional information will still have to be published separately for the time being, and the new legislation will cover third-country bank branches only if they extend reciprocal arrangements to EC banks.

The directive's essential aim is to eliminate unfair discrimination against branches of banks from other EC countries as compared to the host country's domestic bank branches. The directive prohibits Member States from demanding that branches of foreign banks on their territory publish separate branch accounts relating to their activities. Instead, branches will be required to supply the supervisory authorities with copies of the annual report and accounts of their head office. These will have to be drawn up in accordance with the separate Bank Accounts Directive, adopted in 1986. Strict limits and guidelines will be set on the information that foreign bank branches can be required to disclose.

The directive is modeled on the parallel, recently agreed, Eleventh Company Law Directive, which contains similar disclosure rules for foreign branches of companies. The Branches of Banks Directive, however, allows Member States to oblige bank branches to disclose more information than conventional company branches.

The directive establishes a comprehensive list of the information that can be required by the host authorities. In addition to the annual accounts, consolidated accounts, annual report, and opinions of the auditors of the head offices, Member States would be able to oblige foreign bank branches to publish details of their income and costs; claims and liabilities to clients and other credit institutions; total assets and liabilities; and the average number of staff employed by the branch. The list is more extensive than the Commission had originally intended. However, after January 1, 1998, the Commission may submit proposals to eliminate this requirement for additional information in the light of experience acquired in applying the directive and developments in EC banking harmonization.

The directive also includes a reciprocity clause relating to non-EC countries whose bank branches in the EC will benefit from the directive. Member States will be entitled to demand separate branch accounts from third-country bank branches, should the accounts of their head office not be in conformity with or equivalent to accounts drawn up in accordance with the Bank Accounts Directive.

ELECTRONIC PAYMENTS RECOMMENDATIONS

The European Commission's 1985 White Paper announced its intention to put forward proposals concerning electronic banking. A communication published in 1987 outlined the Commission's plans in this area, which are aimed at both ensuring adequate consumer protection and encouraging the interoperability of card bank payment systems on an EC-wide basis.

The Commission's efforts are focused on promoting the benefits of compatible electronic payment systems throughout the internal banking market and encouraging pan-European agreements among banks, retailers, and producers to deal with the problems of network linkage, technical standards, user rules, and protection of card users.

The desired objective is to harmonize differences among the current EC standards for automatic teller machines and electronic funds transfer at point of sale (EFTPOS) terminals, to ensure that cards can be used throughout the EC. The European standardization (CEN) and electrotechnical standardization (CENELEC) bodies have been given the task of drawing up common European standards for payment cards.

In December 1987 the European Commission adopted a recommendation on a code of conduct governing relations among banks issuing payment cards, retailers who install payment terminals in their establishments, and cardholders. In setting out the conditions of fair practice for the various parties concerned, the code calls for the development of compatible electronic payment systems within the EC. By December 31, 1992, EC interoperability should be full and complete, so that traders and consumers can join the network or card issuer of their choice, and each terminal will be able to process all cards.

Interoperability is defined as:

> a state of affairs whereby cards issued in one Member State and/or belonging to a given card system can be used in other Member

> States and/or in the networks installed by other systems. This requires that the cards and readers used in the various systems must be technologically compatible and that systems must be opened up by means of reciprocity agreements.

The code applies to both magnetic strip payment cards and those with a built-in microprocessor ("smart cards"). It defines electronic payment as any payment transaction carried out by means of such cards used at an electronic payment terminal or point of sale terminal. It does not apply to company-specific cards, cards serving purposes other than direct or deferred payment, check guarantee cards, or payments by card using mechanical processes (invoice slips).

The code aims to establish standard terms of contract for the installation of EFTPOS terminals throughout the EC. The essential points are:

- Suppliers of goods and services should be free to choose, purchase, and hire which point of sale terminal they will install.
- Traders should be able, if they wish, to install a single multicard terminal per cash desk, which is capable of accepting all cards.
- Charges should be transparent and freely negotiable.
- Electronic payments should be irrevocable; they may not be countermanded.
- Information in the system databases should be protected.
- There should be interoperability of payment systems.
- EEC Treaty rules on restrictive business practices and abuse of monopoly power should be complied with: contracts between card issuers and traders must contain no exclusive trading clause requiring the traders to operate

only the systems with which they have contracted an agreement.

- All service establishments concerned should be allowed fair access to the different electronic payment systems.

The European Commission adopted a further recommendation in November 1988, addressed to payment card issuers and aimed at establishing minimum EC-wide standards for the protection of consumers in the area of electronic payment systems. It sets out a code of conduct governing the issue of cards, procedures in the event of loss or theft, and consumer liability.

Currently Denmark is the only Member State to have adopted legislation dealing specifically with payment cards. The remaining eleven countries apply their general law of contract and civil liability to regulate matters in this field. The various national rules relating to consumer protection and terms of contract are, however, highly divergent. The consumer's liability in the event of a card being stolen, lost, or copied varies considerably from one Member State to another.

The recommendation thus sets out minimum rules designed to ensure that cardholders receive the same protection in all Member States and that they are correctly informed of the terms of contract and of their rights and obligations under the contract.

The Commission has given card issuers a period of one year in which to incorporate these rules into their standard contracts with consumers. It has been reviewing the situation and is concerned that the banks and retailers are not putting the rules into practice. It appears likely that a proposal to tighten up the rules will be made by replacing the recommendation with a legally binding directive. The Commission had originally proposed a directive but encountered fierce opposition from the banks on the grounds that binding legislation would hold back technological progress in this fast developing area.

The recommendation covers most types of banking transaction and payment, other than cash or check, that are available to the consumer: EFTPOS, withdrawals or deposits at cash dispensing machines and automated teller machines, nonelectronic payment by card (credit cards but not check guarantee cards), and home banking (electronic payment effected by a member of the public without the use of a card). Card issuers are required to:

- Provide full and fair written terms of contract, drafted clearly in easily understandable terms;
- Assume the burden of proof in any dispute with a cardholder. A cardholder who takes all reasonable steps to keep both card and identification number safe and separate should not be held responsible for unauthorized transactions in the event of the card's being lost or stolen;
- Carry liability for the consequences resulting from defects in, or failure of operation of, the cards they issue; such liability may in certain circumstances have to be borne by the issuer jointly with another person or persons, e.g., a retailer and/or a network assembler;
- Provide means whereby their customers may report the loss, theft, or copying of cards 24 hours a day.

In addition, the following rules are laid down:

1. No payment card shall be dispatched to a member of the public unless requested;
2. Manufacturers will have to ensure that the networks, and in particular the equipment containing card-readers, are capable of producing records that enable transactions to be traced and errors to be rectified.

They should also have the facility to supply cardholders with a written record of each transaction.

3. Cardholders will be liable for damage arising out of the loss of their payment cards up to the time they notify the issuer of the loss, but that liability may not exceed 150 ECU. However, this limit does not apply where holders have committed an act of extreme negligence or have behaved fraudulently.

RECOMMENDATION ON CROSS-BORDER TRANSFERS

On February 14, 1990, the European Commission adopted a recommendation on the transparency of banking conditions relating to cross-border financial transactions. EC banks are invited to respect a number of principles aimed at achieving greater transparency in cross-border transfers of funds among Member States. This includes providing customers with easily understandable and accessible information explaining the procedures involved in cross-border financial transactions and giving details of time scales, exchange rates, commission fees, taxes, and any other expected charges. A transfer order will also have to be dealt with within two working days of receipt of the funds and Member States are required to set up independent bodies to handle complaints from dissatisfied users.

PROPOSED REGULATION ON GUARANTEES

The European Commission, on January 15, 1989, proposed a regulation covering guarantees issued by credit institutions or insurance companies. Public authorities would be obligated to accept financial guarantees issued by all banks and insurance companies licensed under EC law. The aims are to ensure freedom to provide services and to counter any discrimination according to nationality or place of establishment in the EC. It would end current practices where guarantees not issued by a domestic bank can be rejected or subjected to additional approval.

Public authorities covered by the proposed regulation include all local or regional government authorities, social security institutions, and law courts; payments covered include those which fall outside the scope of EC law, such as local taxes and rates.

PROPOSED MONEY LAUNDERING DIRECTIVE

In an effort to stem any attempts to take advantage of new opportunities to launder funds connected to criminal activities, presented by the greater freedom of capital movements and financial services, the European Commission put forward a proposal for a directive on February 14, 1990, which would make money laundering a criminal offense throughout the EC, beginning January 1992. The draft directive would oblige banks and other financial institutions to report any transactions suspected to be linked to drugs, terrorism, extortion, and other criminal activities and to keep identification files on all clients. Member States would also have to ensure that banks would not be open to lawsuits for disclosing such information.

6

A Common Market for Insurance Services

The European Commission's legislative program for insurance comprises measures to harmonize the widely differing laws of the Member States relating to supervision and authorization, and to remove any remaining obstacles to the freedom of insurance companies to provide services and establish branches anywhere in the EC. Once again the principle of home country control would be applied. These measures are directed toward achieving a single insurance market in which:

- Insurance companies are free to set up branches throughout the EC;
- Insurers are able to provide insurance services and cover risks throughout the EC without being required to establish branches in the country where the service is provided;
- Insurers are able to operate EC-wide on an equal footing, governed by a similar, regulatory framework;

- Policy holders have access to a wide range of insurance products in an EC-wide market and are furnished with sufficient and comparable information on which to base their choice.

EARLY MOVES TOWARD A SINGLE INSURANCE MARKET

Significant steps have already been taken in the insurance field and a body of EC insurance law built up since 1964 has established the groundwork for freedom of insurance services.

INSURANCE DIRECTIVES ADOPTED PRIOR TO THE 1992 PROGRAMME

Reinsurance Directive 64/225. Abolishes all restrictions on freedom of establishment and freedom to provide services in reinsurance and retrocession.

First Motor Insurance Directive 72/166. Requires Member States to make motor liability insurance compulsory.

First Non-Life Insurance Directive 73/239. Provides a harmonized framework for freedom of establishment in non-life insurance.

Insurance Agents Directive 77/92. Introduces freedom of establishment and freedom to provide services for insurance agents and brokers.

Coinsurance Directive 78/473. Provides for the coinsurance of large risks by insurers in more than one Member State.

First Life Insurance Directive 79/267. Sets out harmonized rules for the freedom of establishment in life insurance.

Second Motor Insurance Directive 84/5. Provides further harmonized rules on compulsory motor insurance.

Assistance Directive 84/641. Amends the first Non-Life Insurance Directive to clarify the extent to which it applies to tourist assistance insurance.

The fundamental First Non-Life Insurance Directive (1973) and its counterpart First Life Insurance Directive (1979) instituted the freedom of establishment (the right to open a subsidiary, branch, or agency in other EC countries) for insurance companies. These directives set out harmonized rules concerning authorization to operate, procedures for setting up branches in other Member States, the legal form of insurance undertakings, cooperation among supervisory authorities, and so forth.

Further directives were adopted covering coinsurance, tourist insurance, motor vehicle liability insurance, and reinsurance. However, progress toward securing the freedom to provide insurance services across EC frontiers has, until recently, been slow.

Court of Justice Rulings

A considerable impetus to this process was provided by important rulings relating to insurance services, delivered by the Court of Justice on December 4, 1986. The Court ruled that host countries could not require insurance undertakings wishing to cover risks situated in their territory to be established there. However, it also drew a clear distinction between those policyholders or insured persons who might be regarded as capable of protecting their own interests ("large risks") and those consumers for whom national protection by the host country was still justified in the present state of EC law ("mass risks").

This judgment paved the way for the adoption of the Second Non-Life Directive, which provided for application of the principle of home country control to large industrial and commercial purchasers of non-life insurance (large risks). Regarding mass risks, the Court ruled that, pending further harmonization, host states were entitled to continue to apply their national regulations governing:

- Technical reserves;
- The nature, spread, and location of assets representing the technical reserves; and
- General and special policy conditions.

Member States were allowed to impose the authorization requirement on insurance companies providing services in their territory until such time as sufficient harmonization had been achieved so that consumers were guaranteed the necessary protection.

Since the Court's ruling, some significant steps have been taken toward the creation of a single insurance market. Three of the proposed directives listed in the European Commission's 1985 White Paper have already been adopted—those relating to credit insurance and legal expenses insurance, as well as the important Second Non-Life Insurance Directive. The remaining proposals, covering such matters as insurance contracts, annual accounts, winding-up, life insurance, and motor vehicle insurance, have all now been tabled.

However, in an address to the Council of Internal Market Ministers on February 22, 1990, Sir Leon Brittan expressed the Commission's concern at the slower pace of progress made in achieving a single insurance market, compared to the more advanced process of liberalization already set in motion in the securities and banking sectors. In order to secure a "level playing field" for the insurance industry, the Commission has announced additional liberalization measures to be proposed during 1990. These include "framework" directives covering non-life and life insurance and a directive on pension funds. The stated intention of the new framework directives is to achieve the single European insurance market by allowing EC insurers to operate EC-wide on the basis of a single insurance license.

CREDIT INSURANCE DIRECTIVE

The Credit Insurance Directive, adopted in 1987, is intended to extend the scope of the First Non-Life Insurance Directive to credit and suretyship insurance companies. Compliance with the directive was required by January 1, 1990.

The directive stipulates that each Member State must require insurance companies established on its territory and underwriting credit risks in credit insurance to set up an equalization reserve. The purpose is to offset any technical deficit or above-average claims ratio arising in that class of insurance for a given financial year. Detailed rules are given on how this equalization reserve should be calculated. Member States have the option of using one of four methods set out in an appendix to the directive, in accordance with their national rules.

Member States would, however, be allowed to exempt insurance companies from the obligation to set up an equalization reserve for credit insurance business where the premiums or contributions receivable in respect of credit insurance are less than 4 percent of the total premiums or contributions receivable, or less than 2,500,000 ECU.

LEGAL EXPENSES DIRECTIVE

A directive to extend the scope of the First Non-Life Insurance Directive to include legal expenses insurance (compensation for injury to the insured party and representation of the injured party in civil, penal, and administrative proceedings) was also adopted in 1987. The purpose of the directive was to coordinate the provisions in the Member States concerning legal expenses, in order to facilitate the effective exercise of freedom of establishment. Member States were given until January 1, 1990 to implement the directive into national law.

Designed to protect the interests of policyholders, the directive also established rules to avoid conflicts of interest when the same company covered both parties involved in a dispute and laid down an arbitration procedure in case of non-agreement.

The following definition of legal expenses insurance is contained in the directive:

> undertaking, against the payment of a premium, to bear the costs of legal proceedings and to provide other services directly linked to insurance cover, with a view to:
>
> - securing compensation for the loss, damage or injury suffered by the insured person, by settlement out of court or through civil or criminal proceedings;
> - defending or representing the insured person in civil, criminal, administrative or other proceedings or in respect of any claim made against him.

The directive imposes the obligation on insurance companies to take all possible precautionary measures to avoid creating any conflicts of interest between a person with legal expenses coverage and his insurer, resulting from the insurer's providing coverage for other insurance classes or for another person. In the event of such a conflict, the company should take steps to enable it to be resolved.

To this end a number of rules require insurers to provide for a separate contract or a separate section of a single policy for legal expenses insurance and stipulate that they either should have separate management for legal expenses insurance or should entrust the management of legal expenses insurance claims to a separate company.

Three alternative solutions are given:

1. The insurance company would ensure that no member of its staff involved in the management of legal expenses claims or the provision of legal advice in this area is simultaneously carrying out similar activities for another class of insurance or in another company that has financial, commercial, or administrative links with the first company, or is engaged in one or more of the other classes of insurance;
2. The company would entrust the management of legal expenses insurance claims to a company with a separate legal identity;
3. The company would specify in the contract that the insured persons are granted the right to entrust the defense of their interests to a lawyer of their choice.

The directive also includes provisions on arbitration procedures, to ensure that any disputes between the insurer and the insured are settled fairly and as rapidly as possible.

SECOND NON-LIFE INSURANCE DIRECTIVE

This directive, which aims to supplement the First Non-Life Insurance Directive so as to allow the freedom to provide services in direct non-life insurance, is the most fundamental of all existing or proposed EC insurance measures. Direct non-life insurance covers insurance in a number of classes defined in an appendix to the First Non-Life Insurance Directive, including insurance against accident, sickness, transport, fire and other property damage, credit, suretyship, and legal expenses, and various liability risks. Adopted in June 1988, after years of deadlock, the Second Non-Life Directive will come into effect after June 30, 1990.

The extension of the home country control principle to non-life insurance means that EC insurance companies will be permitted to cover the risks of large policyholders in any Member State irrespective of where the company is based. Once the directive comes into force they will be able to sell non-life insurance policies directly to large commercial clients throughout the EC without the need to open subsidiaries, agencies, or branches in every EC country, and subject only to the proviso that they have been authorized to operate by their home country regulatory authorities.

This is considered to be a major step toward the creation of a single insurance market and the freedom to provide insurance services across EC frontiers. At present such freedom is permitted by only a few Member States, including the United Kingdom. Some countries do not allow the provision of insurance services by insurers not established in their territory. Others—France, Germany, and Italy for example—actively dissuade their residents from taking out insurance policies outside their home country.

The directive allocates the various regulatory responsibilities between home and host country authorities on the basis of the degree of protection that must be afforded to the policyholder. A distinction is made between "large risks" (policies for commercial and industrial companies) and "mass risks" (policies for smaller policyholders). The extent to which a company would have to observe the regulations of the host country (where the risk is situated) would be greater for mass risks than for large risks.

For large risks, home country control would apply; that is, the insurer's home country regulatory authorities would be largely responsible for supervising its operations.

Large risks are presently defined with reference to the

nature of the risks or the size of the policyholder. After January 1, 1993, large risks will include:

- Transport risks;
- Marine and aviation risks;
- Credit and suretyship risks where the policyholders are carrying on commercial activities;
- Fire and general property damage, general civil liability, and pecuniary loss risks.

The policyholder or group of companies to which the policyholder belongs must meet at least two of the following thresholds:

- 250 employees;
- Turnover of 12.8 million ECU;
- Balance sheet total of 6.2 million ECU.

During a transitional period, from July 1, 1990, until December 31, 1992, the thresholds will be roughly double these figures.

Following the Court of Justice rulings on insurance in December 1986, mass risks (smaller policyholders), considered to need extra protection, were excluded from the provisions on home country control. Instead, the country where the services were being provided was entitled to impose a requirement on the insurer to be authorized in the host state and to comply with local regulations on such matters as technical reserves and general and special policy conditions.

The European Commission is aiming to achieve full freedom of services, based on home country control, for the smaller policyholders as well. A proposal is due to be tabled during the first half of 1990 for a framework directive that will extend this freedom to mass risks.

Choice of the Law Governing Contracts

Another key provision contained in the directive concerns the choice of the law applicable to the insurance contract. Insurance contract law differs considerably from one Member State to another. In certain specific circumstances, the directive would provide for the freedom to choose, as the law applicable to the contract, a law other than that of the Member State in which the risk is situated.

Rules are detailed on how the law of the contract should be determined and the degree of choice that is permitted. The aim is to ensure that policyholders never find themselves in the position where a contract law is applied with which they have no apparent connection.

Premium Taxes

The situation regarding premium taxation varies considerably among the EC Member States. Some do not subject insurance transactions to any form of indirect taxation while the majority apply special taxes with highly divergent structures and rates. The European Commission would like to eliminate potential distortions of competition in insurance services among Member States resulting from these existing differences.

However, pending future harmonization, it has been agreed that the Member State where the risk is situated will be entitled to charge its own premium taxes and use its own system of tax collection, irrespective of whether the insurer covering the risk is established in the Member State.

Transitional Arrangements

Spain, Portugal, Ireland, and Greece have been granted temporary derogations from the directive, to allow their less developed insurance industries more time to prepare themselves for the expected onslaught of increased competition resulting from the liberalization of non-life insurance. They will not have to open up their currently protected industries to the rigors of equal competition from other EC insurers until the end of 1992.

The adoption of the Second Non-Life Insurance Directive is, however, viewed as only a modest step toward the creation of a single market in insurance. The Commission is attaching a high priority to speeding up this process through the introduction of further legislative proposals in 1990. The new framework directive for non-life insurance is expected to be drafted during the first half of 1990. It will introduce a single insurance license to allow insurance companies the freedom to set up branches and sell policies for mass risks. In other EC countries subject to home country control. The non-life framework directive will also include provisions dealing with contract law and policy conditions, and taxation of insurance companies and policy premiums. Existing restrictions on "composite" companies (those which transact both life and non-life insurance business) are also likely to be eased.

PROPOSED INSURANCE CONTRACTS DIRECTIVE

This proposed directive is intended to coordinate the national laws of the Member States governing insurance contracts for non-life insurance. Originally proposed in 1979 and later amended in 1980, it has been under discussion for years.

The draft directive is concerned with the declaration of risks by the policyholders; information to be included in the contract; the principle of proportionality; the concepts of "reasonableness," the "prudent insurer," and "constructive knowledge"; and termination of contracts. It is closely related to the Second Non-Life Insurance Directive, which contains detailed provisions concerning freedom of choice in the law of the contract.

There has been speculation that the need for a separate insurance contracts directive might now have been superseded since the rules set out in the Second Non-Life Insurance Directive have essentially the same aim: to minimize the chances of a policyholder's coming up against unfamiliar or unconnected contract law. The Commission has recently stated that it will either withdraw or substantially amend the insurance contracts proposal.

PROPOSED DIRECTIVE ON THE ANNUAL ACCOUNTS OF INSURANCE COMPANIES

This proposed directive, which has been under discussion since December 1986, is designed to harmonize layout and valuation rules to be used in drawing up the annual accounts of insurance companies as well as the consolidated accounts of groups of insurance companies.

The directive's aim is to establish a system of accounting by insurance companies that allows for improved comparability throughout the Member States, so as to assist creditors, debtors, prospective policyholders and their advisors, and the general public and to encourage fair conditions of competition among EC insurance companies.

Prospective policyholders will have access to standard, comprehensive information on the financial situation of insurance companies situated anywhere in the EC.

Currently the structure and content of the balance sheets of insurance companies in the various Member States are appreciably different. The proposed directive seeks to establish a uniform structure and the same item designations for the balance sheets of all EC insurance companies. It would also harmonize requirements regarding the presentation of certain transactions in the balance sheet, the content of certain balance sheet items, and the composition and definition of certain items in the profit and loss account.

The proposed text is highly technical and detailed, and aims to adapt the provisions of the Fourth Directive on company accounts and the Seventh Directive on consolidated accounts to the particular needs of the insurance industry.

The proposal sets out rules governing:

- The layout of the balance sheet
- Special provisions relating to certain balance sheet items
- The layout of the profit and loss account
- The contents of the notes to the accounts
- Consolidated accounts
- The publication of annual accounts and annual reports

To facilitate comparability throughout the EC, the proposal also contains provisions covering the values at which assets and liabilities are entered in the balance sheet. Companies must disclose the current value of investments as well as their value at a time in the past. The essential aim of the Commission's proposal is to permit companies to use either the current or historical methods of evaluation, provided that the results of the method not used are recorded in the notes to the accounts.

In March 1989 the European Parliament proposed a major amendment that would remove the obligation to state in notes to the accounts the current value figures which are drawn up using the historical value method. A revised proposal, produced on October 25, 1989, makes a number of changes to the original version. These are principally concerned with Lloyd's, the gross and net presentation in the profit and loss account, and the presentation of commissions.

The Commission was, however, unable to agree to Parliament's proposed amendments to the valuation rules, since the use of the historical method allows a company to undervalue its assets and so build up significant "hidden reserves." This would be contrary to the Commission's policy of providing the consumer with sufficient and transparent information upon which to make effective comparisons.

To resolve the question over whether Lloyd's as a whole or Lloyd's and its constituent parts should be obliged to render accounts, the new text includes an amendment, proposed by the Parliament, which provides that the Lloyd's syndicates are also accountable in principle.

PROPOSED DIRECTIVE ON THE WINDING-UP OF INSURANCE COMPANIES

Dating back to 1986, and amended on September 12, 1989, the intention of this proposal is to harmonize the provisions of Member States in the event of a company's going bankrupt or having its authorization to operate withdrawn. The proposal aims to provide a guarantee for insurance company creditors, through a single, EC-wide procedure, of equal treatment when an insurance company is wound up. By dispelling one of the fears that could deter a resident of one Member State from considering an insurance policy with a company established in another Member State, the proposal helps to increase the confidence of policyholders.

Compulsory winding-up is the automatic consequence of the withdrawal of authorization. The proposed directive draws a distinction between "normal compulsory winding-up," where the undertaking is solvent, and "special compulsory winding-up," where it is not.

Harmonized rules are given, relating to:

- The duties of the supervisory authorities
- Insurance contracts in the event of a company's being wound up
- The distribution of assets in the event of insolvency

These rules are designed to ensure that, in such circumstances, there is no discrimination against creditors in the division of assets on the grounds of nationality, residence, or place of the conclusion of the contract.

The proposal establishes the principle that a proportion of a liquidated company's assets corresponding to its "technical reserves" must be reserved for repaying debts to policyholders. If adopted, companies will be required to maintain sufficient technical reserves, covered by equivalent and matching assets, localized in each country where the company operates. Certain Member States, for example the United Kingdom, would have to alter their practices, since they presently make no distinction between technical reserves and other assets when a company goes into liquidation.

Every company will have to keep registers, in each Member State where it has its head office or an agency or branch, of the assets representing the technical reserves corresponding to direct insurance transactions. The total value of the assets entered into the register will have to be equal to or greater than the value of the technical reserves.

Detailed provisions regarding the procedure to be followed in the case of special compulsory winding-up govern such matters as:

- The appointment of liquidators and assistant liquidators
- The transfer of portfolios
- The termination of non-life insurance contracts
- Life insurance contracts

The assets entered in the registers would be realized and the proceeds distributed. The proposed directive sets an order of priority for eligible claims for non-life and life insurance business. Its provisions apply to agencies or branches of third-country companies established in the territory of the Community.

The proposal states that:

> The normal and compulsory winding-up of an undertaking shall take effect in all Member States. It shall preclude the opening of any other winding-up procedure in respect of an agency or branch of the undertaking situated in another Member State.

This is known as the "unity/universality principle": the bankruptcy of a company is interpreted as applying in all Member States where the debtor has creditors, as compared with the territoriality principle whereby a debtor may be declared bankrupt in each country in which its insolvency is established.

At present, France applies the principle of territoriality, which involves separately establishing insolvency in each individual Member State where the company operates. Other Member States, such as the United Kingdom, Germany, Italy, and the Netherlands, take account of both the territoriality and universality principles; Luxembourg, Belgium, and Denmark apply only the universality concept.

In March 1989, the European Parliament proposed some minor amendments that were incorporated into a revised version of the proposal. The changes relate to the advertising of winding-up in national papers and the wording of articles on "normal" and "special" compulsory winding-up. The Parliament has also requested the Commission to examine the possibility of drawing up a European Community Insurance Code in place of the complex network of interlacing insurance legislation currently being created.

PROPOSED LIFE INSURANCE DIRECTIVE

This proposal for the life insurance sector amends the 1979 First Life Insurance Directive, which coordinated the conditions under which a life insurance company from one Member State may set up an agency or branch in another Member State, thus providing for freedom of establishment. The new proposed directive seeks to lay down provisions relating specifically to freedom to provide services in life insurance.

Proposed on December 23, 1988, it is aimed at allowing insurers the freedom to exercise the right to cover life insurance risks through the provision of services across frontiers. It is modeled on the parallel Second Non-Life Insurance Directive and contains several similar or identical provisions.

On December 21, 1989, the Council reached political agreement on the life insurance proposal. However, before a formalized common position can be adopted, the European Commission must first approve a revised draft produced on March 1, 1990, so that the European Parliament may deliver its opinion and complete the first reading of the proposal. The text agreed by the Council incorporates a number of important changes including the addition of group coverage within the scope of the directive and provisions relating to the role of brokers, advertising and reciprocity with third countries.

The European Commission is following a similar approach to that adopted for the Second Non-Life Insurance Directive. The proposed directive makes a distinction between policyholders who are in no great need of protection, for whom the home country rules will apply, and other policyholders who require a greater degree of protection, for whom the host country rules will apply.

Unlike the Second Non-Life Insurance Directive, this distinction is made, not according to the size of the client, but on the basis of whether the client has taken the initiative to approach a life insurance company in another Member State.

Own Initiative

Once adopted, the directive will give prospective policyholders the right to seek individual life insurance in other Member States by approaching a life company on their own initiative. Currently the laws of many Member States forbid residents to take out a life insurance policy abroad, even when acting on their own initiative.

The Directive states that persons who take the initiative in approaching an insurer established in another EC country or a broker in order to obtain information on insurance contracts offered by insurance companies in other EC countries, must first sign a formal statement taking note of the fact that the policy is subject to the supervisory rules of the country of the insurer. Restrictions on advertising by insurers and brokers have been removed from the amended text. However, national protection will still apply where insurers actively seek to sell their products abroad.

Where Policyholders Require Special Protection

If a life insurance company actively canvasses for customers in another Member State, that country will be entitled to require the company to be authorized by its supervisory authorities and to meet certain local rules on such matters as technical reserves and conditions of insurance. This authorization requirement may be imposed in circumstances where it is necessary in the public interest to protect the insured persons.

Before authorization is granted the foreign insurer may be required to produce various documents such as a certificate of solvency, a certificate of authorization, and a business plan. The country in which the service is being provided may also insist that the information being provided is in conformity with the laws and regulations applicable in its territory, notably as regards technical reserves, including mathematical reserves, and the assets representing those reserves.

A new framework directive for life insurance, due to be tabled by the end of 1990, will introduce home country supervision even when the insurer actively canvasses for customers in another Member State.

One aspect of the original draft aroused some controversy: it excluded composite offices (those transacting both life and non-life insurance) from its scope. British insurers in particular were concerned that this might introduce new obstacles to cross-border freedom of services since in several Member States it is already possible for residents to purchase life insurance at either composite or exclusive life insurance offices in other Member States, provided that they act on their own initiative. A more flexible regime has now been introduced in the revised text.

Reciprocity

The life insurance proposal's rules, requiring reciprocal access to third countries' life insurance markets before non-EC firms can be established in the EC, are similar to those featured in the Second Banking Coordination Directive. These provide for procedures for negotiating with third countries and, as a last resort, for the possibility of taking measures involving the suspension of new applications for authorization by non-EC insurers, to operate in the single European life insurance market. The reciprocity regime would apply if a third country does not provide EC insurers with effective market access comparable to that offered by the EC, or national treatment offering the same competitive opportunities as to insurers of that third country. (This is described in more detail on page 76.)

Taxation

The taxation of premiums and its budgetary impact raise several questions. Rates range between 0 and 5.15 percent: Germany, the UK, the Netherlands, and Spain apply a zero rating; other countries apply rates of 2, 2.4 and 4.4 percent; and France applies various rates ranging from 0 percent for group insurance schemes to 5.15 percent for individuals.

The life insurance proposal, in line with the Second Non-Life Insurance Directive, does not aim to harmonize the taxation of premiums, but pending further harmonization, opts for the territoriality principle whereby the tax rates and collection arrangements of the country of the policyholder are applied.

Pension schemes are not covered by the directive because of the multiplicity and complexity of the various schemes and their close relationship to social security. These are to be the subject of a separate pension funds directive to be proposed in 1990. It will be aimed at securing full freedom of cross-border marketing of private retirement benefits, freedom of management services, and the possibility of creating an EC-wide pension fund.

PROPOSED MOTOR VEHICLE INSURANCE DIRECTIVE—FREEDOM TO PROVIDE SERVICES

This proposal brings third-party motor vehicle insurance within the scope of the Second Non-Life Insurance Directive and at the same time draws the distinction between large risks and small risks in this class of insurance.

Proposed on December 16, 1988, it seeks to secure the freedom to provide services in auto insurance throughout the EC by applying the rules of the Second Non-Life Insurance

Directive to both compulsory third-party auto insurance and optional cover (essentially insurance for damage to or theft of the insured's own vehicle). The principle of home country control will apply to motor vehicle policies taken out by larger industrial and commercial concerns ("large risks" as defined in the Second Directive). Insurers covering third-party risk in such cases will be exempted from the requirement to be authorized by the host state.

Compulsory motor vehicle insurance was originally excluded from the Second Non-Life Insurance Directive, which deals specifically with freedom of services, because of special problems in this area. These relate to:

- The operation of the national guarantee funds (set up to compensate the victims of uninsured or unidentified vehicles)
- The operation of the green card system (agreements between the national motor insurers' bureaus), and in particular of the Supplementary Agreement between national motor insurers' bureaus
- The need to safeguard the interests of accident victims in their position as third-party claimants

The objectives of the proposal are to allow prospective motor vehicle insurance buyers access to a wider choice of potential insurers and to encourage more effective competition in this field while at the same time safeguarding the interests of accident victims.

The proposal inserts an article that allows risks in motor vehicle liability, and damage to or loss of land motor vehicles, to be treated as large risks, effectively cancelling their exclusion from the freedom to provide services provisions contained in the Second Non-Life Insurance Directive.

The European Commission believes that an insurer covering the liability of a vehicle bearing the registration plate of a given Member State should be obliged to join and participate in the financing of the bureau in that country. Currently all motor vehicle insurers in the different Member States are required to belong to and finance the national bureau in their home country. The bureau gives a guarantee to other participating bureaus that it will accept financial liability for accidents caused by a vehicle from its own country and occurring in the countries of the other bureaus. Under this system the bureau in the country where the accident takes place can pay out compensation knowing that it will be reimbursed by the bureau of the country to which the vehicle belongs.

This direct link between the vehicle's home country and the insurer's membership of the bureau in that country would, however, cease to exist once the freedom to provide motor vehicle insurance services across borders is introduced under the proposed directive. The Commission recognizes in its proposal that a Member State would no longer be able to give an unconditional guarantee for all vehicles registered in its territory, having no certainty that any given vehicle was insured by a member insurer of its national bureau and having no financial commitment from a nonmember insurer. Without this guarantee the bureaus of other Member States would hesitate to compensate victims.

For this reason a new clause is inserted which stipulates that the Member State where the insurance services are provided should oblige the insurance company offering the service to become a member of and participate in the financing of its national auto insurers' bureau. The membership premium, in line with existing practice, will be based on the premium income derived from this insurance class in the country concerned or on the number of vehicles insured. An annual membership fee or minimum contribution that bears no relation to the amount of business transacted in that country would act as a considerable deterrent for any company covering a small number of risks or receiving a small premium income in this class of insurance.

The Commission believes that insurers should also be obliged to join and contribute to the financing of the local guarantee fund in the country where they are offering their services. Member States are required by an existing directive to have a guarantee fund to ensure that accident victims are not left without compensation in the event that the party responsible for an accident is uninsured or unidentified.

In order to avoid placing third-party claimants at a disadvantage when dealing with a "services" insurer as opposed to an insurer established in the country, the new article allows the host country to require the insurance company providing services to nominate a claims settlement representative in that country. The representative, who could be an employee of the insurance company, would have to limit his or her activities on its behalf to the handling and settlement of claims.

On February 14, 1990, the European Parliament delivered its first opinion on the proposal and called for some substantial amendments. In direct contradiction to the basic aims of the directive, it proposed that even companies should be offered the protection of their domestic laws when seeking a policy in another EC country: An insurer wishing to sell a motor vehicle policy in another Member State would therefore have to observe the national regulations of the host country where the risk is situated. The aim of the Parliament's proposed amendments is to ensure that priority is given to protecting the interests of the potential accident victim, not the policyholder. The Commission has, however, rejected this suggestion and the proposal must now be resubmitted for consideration by the Council.

PROPOSED THIRD DIRECTIVE ON MOTOR VEHICLE INSURANCE

A new proposal, for a Third Motor Liability Insurance Directive, put forward on December 20, 1988, is directed toward resolving any problems and filling any gaps left over from the first and second motor vehicle insurance directives (1972 and 1983), and improving the insurance coverage afforded to motorists throughout the EC. Scheduled to be adopted in 1990, the proposed date of implementation is December 31, 1992.

The first and second directives enabled green card insurance checks to be abolished and began the process of reducing the disparities between the levels and content of compulsory third-party motor vehicle insurance in the Member States.

The draft Third Motor Liability Insurance Directive establishes the principle of EC-wide motor vehicle insurance coverage based on a standard premium, which would afford protection to motorists in all EC countries without the need to pay an additional charge. It also seeks to define clearly the minimum, compulsory, third-party coverage that an insurance company must provide; the entitlement of accident victims to claim compensation; and the obligations of insurance companies under the guarantee fund, for damage caused by uninsured drivers. Its rules ensure that a victim will be compensated as rapidly as possible, where disputes arise over whether the guarantee fund or the insurer should pay damages.

Passenger Coverage

The European Commission is aware of gaps that still exist in passenger coverage in various Member States (see Table 6-1). Greece still has no compulsory passenger coverage (but is planning to introduce it), Ireland and Luxembourg do not at present require insurance coverage for liability toward motorcycle

Table 6–1
Compulsory Motor Insurance in the Member States at January 1, 1989

Member State	Personal Injuries per Event		Personal Injuries per Person		Property Damage	
	Currency	*ECU*	*Currency*	*ECU*	*Currency*	*ECU*
Belgium	Unlimited		Unlimited		Unlimited except for fire and explosion: FB 5 million	115,940
Denmark	Dkr 60 million	7,514,136	Dkr 50 million	6,261,780	Dkr 10 million	1,252,356
Germany	DM 1.5 million	721,848	DM 1 million	481,232	DM 400,000	192,493
Greece	DR 10 million	62,965	—		DR 2 million	12,593
Spain	—		Ptas 8 million	58,024	Ptas 2.2 million	15,957
France	—		FF 5 million	722,871	FF 3 million	433,723
Ireland	Unlimited		Unlimited		£IRL 40,000	51,672
Italy	LIT 500 million	333,544	LIT 300 million	200,127	LIT 50 million	35,355
Luxembourg	Unlimited		Unlimited		Unlimited except for fire and explosion: FL 50 million	1,159,396
Netherlands	FL 2 million (including property damage)	855,334				
Portugal	Esc. 20 million (including property damage)	122,236	Esc. 12 million (including property damage)	73,342		
United Kingdom	Unlimited		Unlimited		£ST 250,000	360,288

Source: Commission of the European Communities

Notes: ECU conversion rates as of September 30, 1987 (amounts rounded up or down to nearest ECU).
France, Germany, Italy, the Netherlands, and Portugal apply higher amounts for certain vehicle categories.
Greece and Italy apply lower amounts for all or certain motorcycles.

passengers, and several Member States exclude the policyholder or owner of the vehicle even when not driving the vehicle but carried as a passenger. EC residents traveling as passengers in a locally registered vehicle, when visiting another Member State, often are unclear about the insurance coverage provided and are subject to the compulsory motor vehicle insurance coverage of the country visited.

The proposal's aim is to assure EC citizens traveling anywhere in the EC of equivalent protection when carried as passengers. The proposal states that all passengers, other than a driver or passengers who have knowingly and willingly entered a stolen vehicle, must be afforded the protection of third-party insurance cover.

EC-Wide Coverage

In some Member States policyholders must notify their insurer and pay an additional premium, if they wish to take their vehicle to another Member State. The proposal states that this requirement should be discontinued and that every third-party motor vehicle insurance policy should provide coverage throughout the EC on the basis of a single premium and should guarantee at least the minimum coverage legally required in each Member State.

Guarantee Fund

The second motor vehicle insurance directive requires Member States to have a guarantee fund to compensate the victims of uninsured or hit-and-run vehicles. However, in certain Member States, before the victims of an accident caused by an uninsured driver can claim on the guarantee fund they must first prove that they are unable to obtain compensation from the uninsured driver. This means establishing that the party responsible is unwilling or unable to pay compensation, which can result in the victims' having to resort to taking legal action. The Commission believes that in such cases the guarantee fund should pay compensation to the victims as soon as the liability of the uninsured driver is established on the grounds that the guarantee fund is better placed than victims, particularly visiting victims, to defend its interests.

The proposal therefore stipulates that the guarantee fund must not require victims first to prove that the uninsured party responsible is unable or unwilling to pay compensation.

Disputes

Another problem can arise with nonpayment of the premium, where there is a doubt as to whether it should be the insurer or the guarantee fund that compensates the victims. To protect the interests of the victims, and avoid delay in the payment of compensation, the draft directive requires that either the insurer or the fund should be designated as the payer of first instance until the dispute is resolved.

An amended proposal was produced on December 6, 1989, which included a number of changes. These are designed to ensure that motorists using their vehicles outside their home states will never have less than their home state insurance coverage and also to introduce a more flexible solution to the problem raised by a dispute between an insurer and the guarantee fund. On December 15, 1989, a common position was adopted on the proposal and the European Parliament will now have to deliver its second opinion before the directive can be adopted by the Council.

7

Toward an Integrated Market in Securities

The integration of the EC's securities markets is another major goal in the European Commission's plans for the financial services sector. The 1985 White Paper recognized the need for companies and investors to be able to obtain finance and choose investment products on an EC-wide basis in a single European market.

As with its proposals for the banking sector, the Commission's principal objective is to establish a single regulatory framework for the investment and securities industries, based on the central concepts of home country control and a single license to operate throughout the EC. The related goals are: to give investors confidence to invest in other Member States; to make it easier for companies to place their securities on stock exchanges anywhere in the EC; to afford investors minimum guarantees of protection in all Member States; and to provide investors with sufficient and accurate information on which to base their investment decisions. Proposed investment measures are thus directed at coordinating rules in such areas as stock exchange listing, unit trusts, public offer prospectuses, and major shareholdings.

STOCK EXCHANGE DIRECTIVES

Some progress has already been made toward the integration of the EC's securities markets. A number of directives dealing with official stock exchange listing are already in place. These include the 1979 Admissions Directive 79/279, which aimed to harmonize the minimum conditions for the admission of securities to official quotation on stock exchanges in the Member States, and the 1982 Interim Reports Directive 82/121, which covered the financial information to be published on a regular basis by companies whose securities are admitted to listing on a stock exchange.

Another key directive is the Listing Particulars Directive 80/390, adopted on March 17, 1980, which promulgated rules on the minimum listing particulars to be published before securities can be officially quoted on stock exchanges. Its purpose was to eliminate differences among Member States' requirements for the drawing-up, scrutiny, and distribution of listing particulars so as to achieve an adequate degree of equivalent investor protection. The directive stipulated that listing particulars must contain the information that is necessary to enable investors and their advisors to make an informed assessment of the assets and liabilities, financial position, profits and losses, and prospects of the issuer and of the rights attaching to such securities.

Amended Listing Particulars Directive

An amendment to the Listing Particulars Directive, adopted on June 22, 1987, makes it easier for companies to obtain multinational listings throughout the EC. This coincided with the abolition, effective as of March 1987, of exchange control restrictions on the admission of securities to official stock exchange listing, as decreed by a 1960 directive on liberalization of capital movements. (See page 154.)

The amended directive, which was due to become effective January 1, 1990, applies the principle of mutual recognition to listing particulars. A company wishing to apply for official listing on stock exchanges in more than one Member State will be able to draw up listing particulars for only one exchange, provided that its listing particulars have been approved by the supervisory authorities in one Member State. (Currently the information required to be published for admission to listing on stock exchanges varies from Member State to Member State.) The directive sets out rules to determine which Member State's legislation is to apply, regarding the content and approval of the listing particulars, and provides for cooperation among the relevant authorities of the Member States.

The benefits of mutual recognition of listing particulars will be extended to non-EC countries subject to reciprocal agreements being concluded between the EC and the countries concerned.

The adoption of this directive will mean important changes for some stock exchanges in the EC. London, for instance, where listing rules are among the most stringent in Europe, is proposing to ease its requirement for a five-year trading record from companies seeking a listing on its main market to the three-year qualifying period demanded elsewhere in the EC. In addition, the International Stock Exchange has decided to phase out the Third Market.

THE UCITS DIRECTIVE

This directive on Undertakings for Collective Investment in Transferable Securities (UCITS), adopted in December, 1985, covers unit trust companies and investment companies, and the information to be supplied to the unit holders. The directive, allowing open-ended funds to be marketed across borders in the EC, was due to be implemented into national legislation on October 1, 1989, with transitional arrangements for Greece and Portugal.

UCITS are defined as "undertakings the sole object of which is the collective investment in transferable securities of capital raised from the public and which operate on the principle of risk-spreading" and "the units of which are, at the request of holders, repurchased or redeemed, directly or indirectly, out of those undertakings' assets."

The directive does not apply to closed-end UCITS, which do not promote the sale of their units to the public; these will be the subject of coordination at a later stage.

The purpose of the directive is to coordinate national laws governing UCITS so as to allow investment undertakings to compete on an equal basis throughout the EC while at the same time ensuring more effective and more uniform protection for unit holders. Its essential aim is to make it easier for a UCITS established in one Member State to market units in other Member States by eliminating obstacles to the free circulation of unit trusts in the EC. By applying the home country control principle, a UCITS authorized to operate by its home country authorities will be entitled to market its units anywhere in the EC without further approval by other Member States' authorities.

For an authorization granted by one Member State to be recognized by the competent authorities of the other Member States, it must meet the directive's basic rules on the authorization, supervision, structure, and activities of UCITS and the information they must publish. These relate to:

- The structure of unit trusts
- The structure of investment companies and their depositaries

- The investment policies of UCITS
- The information to be supplied to unit holders (publication of prospectuses and periodical reports)
- The general obligations of UCITS

Once authorized by its home Member State, a UCITS intending to market its units in another Member State will be required to notify both its home regulatory authority and the authorities of the country where it is intending to offer its services. It will then be able to commence its activities in the host country two months after this notification procedure has been followed.

Member States are required to nominate the competent authorities that will be responsible for carrying out the duties of authorization and supervision, and these tasks are allocated between home and host regulators. The home country authorities will thus have the responsibility of supervising the operations of the UCITS while, as an exception to the home country control principle, the authorities of the host state in which it markets its units will be empowered to enforce local advertising and marketing rules.

The directive specifies what types of investments are allowed and sets limits on concentrated investment by a UCITS in the same body. A clear distinction is made between transferable securities that are issued or guaranteed by a state and those that are not. For the latter, the directive stipulates that a UCITS may invest no more than 5 percent of its assets in transferable securities issued by the same body. The limit on a fund's investment in state-issued securities is, however, raised to a maximum of 35 percent of the fund's assets.

These limits were intended to lessen the risks of adverse effects which a possible bankruptcy or cessation of payments could have on the assets of a UCITS. However, the directive did not take recognition of the fact that other types of bonds, like Danish mortgage credit bonds, may offer guarantees similar to those of state bonds. This would, for instance, be the case where there is little risk of the issuer's becoming bankrupt or where protection is guaranteed in the event of the issuer's ceasing payment.

Amending Directive

In March 1988 the UCITS directive was therefore amended to incorporate the principle of treating certain bonds as equivalent to state bonds where they offer similar guarantees. It is left to the Member States to draw up themselves the lists of bonds which they would include in this category.

The Liberalization of UCITS

Another directive, adopted at the same time as the 1985 UCITS Directive, provides for the liberalization of capital movements associated with UCITS so as to remove the restrictions on cross-border transactions in unit trusts.

PROPOSED INVESTMENT SERVICES DIRECTIVE

At the core of the European Commission's plans for an integrated securities market is its proposal for an Investment Services Directive aimed at opening up the market in financial services in the non-banking sector. Published in December 1988, and later amended in January 1990, it will, if adopted, allow authorized investment firms the freedom to provide investment services across frontiers or to establish branches throughout the EC. Investment services are defined as any of the instruments listed in an appendix to the draft directive (see page 135).

The proposed directive, to take effect in 1993, aims to establish a broad EC framework for the regulation of the investment industry and to liberalize access to membership of EC stock exchanges and financial futures and options exchanges. This would permit authorized investment firms to have access to membership of host Member States' exchanges either directly by setting up a branch in the host state or indirectly by setting up a subsidiary or by acquisition of an existing firm. Firms would also be able to gain electronic access to membership without the need to have an establishment in the host state.

Like the banking directive, it is founded on the principles of home country control and the concept of a single license for investment firms to operate EC-wide. Prior harmonization of essential rules governing authorization procedures and supervisory systems will be required.

In essence this means that any securities firm that has been authorized to operate in its home country would effectively receive a passport to offer its services or establish branches anywhere in the EC without the need to obtain further authorization.

The directive is aimed at nonbanking institutions that engage in investment activities and is the counterpart in the securities sector of the second banking directive, offering parallel freedoms to securities houses which do not form part of a banking group. Banks will not be required to file for additional authorization to offer investment services EC-wide; they will already be licensed to do so by the banking directive.

The two directives are intended to complement each other. Many of the provisions for investment services are closely modeled on the banking directive, and the list of securities-related activities which they cover is similar. The revised draft, produced in January 1990, contains several amendments relating to clauses that have been reworded to reflect the approach adopted in the banking directive. Parallel rules laid down in the investment services proposal would regulate such matters as professional secrecy, future updating of the directive, the suitability of shareholders, reciprocity, and authorization procedures. The Commission envisages that both will take effect at the same time so as to ensure a level playing field between banks and securities houses and to prevent banks from being granted the new freedoms first, at the expense of investment firms.

Obtaining the Single License

The directive sets out the authorization procedure which an investment firm must follow in order to secure the single license. Each Member State will be required to nominate one or more home regulatory authorities to grant authorizations, subject to essential minimum conditions being met. Investment firms whose existing authorization already meets the directive's standards will not have to be authorized again when the directive comes into force.

Authorization will be dependent on the following criteria:

- Sufficient initial financial resources
- Suitability of the major shareholders; directors must be of sufficiently good repute and experience
- Compliance with prudential rules
- Continued financial soundness

The directive does not stipulate a fixed minimum amount of initial financial resources needed; this will vary depending on the nature of the investment service to be provided. Additional rules relating to the capital to be set aside by investment firms to cover market risk are set out in a separate capital adequacy directive proposed on April 25, 1990.

An investment firm that is authorized in one Member

State and wishes to set up branches or provide services in another Member State will be required to deliver its request for authorization to the home country authority. Applications for authorization will have to be accompanied by a business plan describing the types of business envisaged and the structural organization of the investment firm. Applicants will be notified within three months of submission whether authorization is granted.

Once authorization has been obtained from the home country regulator, a firm will have the right to engage in a wide range of investment activities, provided it is permitted to offer these services in its home country. An appendix to the draft directive lists the range of investment activities which the firm would be able to offer in other EC countries. These include:

- Brokerage
- Dealing as principal
- Market making
- Portfolio management
- Professional investment advice
- Underwriting transferable securities and UCITS (unit trusts)
- Safekeeping and administration

A separate list also gives the nature of investments covered:

- Transferable securities
- Money market instruments
- Financial futures and options
- Exchange rates and interest rate instruments

Home Country Control

The emphasis would be on home regulation; in other words, the designated home regulatory authority would have the task of supervising the operations of the securities firm and the host country authorities would have a complementary role.

In addition to granting authorization, the home country supervisors would be responsible for monitoring the financial soundness of the investment firm and ensuring its compliance with a number of prudential rules. These rules relate to:

- Administrative and accounting procedures and internal control mechanisms
- Arrangements for keeping investors' money and securities separate from those of the firm
- Compensation for investors against loss resulting from bankruptcy or default of the firm
- Information for the competent authorities of the home Member State
- Record-keeping
- Management of conflicts of interest

Rules that govern the relationship between investment firms and their clients (conduct of business rules) are exempt from home country control. These rules vary considerably from Member State to Member State and the European Commission believes that significant harmonization will be required in order to allow them to pass under the control of the home country authorities. Pending such further harmonization they will continue to be enforced by the host country authorities, provided that they can be justified on the grounds of "general good." There is a possibility that a directive to coordinate conduct of business rules may be produced in the long term, but in the meantime the European Commission has adopted a "wait and see" approach in the hope that market forces may in due course lead to a natural process of convergence.

In addition, the directive on investment services provides that host countries may, in emergencies, take measures necessary to protect the interests of investors and others.

As with the banking directive, the home country control concept has prompted concern that British firms, for example, which are subject to a more stringent home regime, could be placed at a competitive disadvantage in relation to firms from Luxembourg, for instance, which are lightly regulated. In a single financial market, given that the degree of regulation varies considerably from one Member State to another, investors would be able to choose between more strictly or more lightly regulated firms. Moreover, highly regulated markets like the United Kingdom are worried that firms may opt to move or set up their headquarters in Member States with less stringent authorization requirements.

As a further consequence of the proposed new legislation, securities firms that are not authorized in their home country to provide some of the listed services will find themselves at a competitive disadvantage compared with firms from other Member States that are able to provide the full range.

Reciprocity

At the heart of the debate surrounding the Investment Services Directive has been a reciprocity clause intended to ensure that EC investment firms are granted reciprocal treatment in third countries. Entry to the single market for non-EC firms will be conditional on their home country's allowing reciprocal access to its markets to EC firms.

It was initially proposed that requests for authorization of a third-country subsidiary should be subjected to a reciprocity test similar to that originally envisaged in the first draft of the banking directive: The competent authorities of the relevant Member State would have to inform the authorities of the other Member States and the European Commission of the request. Authorization would be withheld while the Commission examined whether all EC investment firms enjoyed "reciprocal treatment" in the third country concerned. If reciprocity is not ensured, authorization would be further suspended, pending negotiations into securing suitable reciprocal arrangements.

As with the second banking directive, the reciprocity provisions have been softened in the revised draft to require in essence that the non-EC state grant "effective market access" to EC investment firms. The new reciprocity test now mirrors the procedure agreed upon for the second banking directive. (See page 78.)

This reciprocity regime will not act retrospectively; that is, it will not apply to existing investment firms already operating in the EC prior to the date on which the directive takes effect on January 1, 1993. This should give sufficient time for foreign investment firms wishing to set up a subsidiary within the EC in order to benefit from the single passport.

The reciprocity clause has major implications for the UK in particular which, as an international financial center, hosts a large number of foreign securities houses from countries outside the EC. The UK is unhappy about the possibility that a third country which does not grant reciprocal rights to another Member State—Spain, for example—could in theory also be denied access to the UK.

Another area to note concerns the status of branches as compared to subsidiaries. Under the directive, a branch of a non-EC investment firm located in a Member State will not be eligible for EC home country authorization and will not therefore automatically be entitled to provide cross-border investment services or to establish branches in other Member States. This is also the position under the second banking directive.

Under EC law, a firm must be "established" in a Member State in order to be eligible for the single passport treatment. Branches or agencies are not considered to be established, but subsidiaries of non-EC firms normally pass the test of establishment, unless their economic links with the EC are tenuous or very short-term. It is important for non-EC investment firms that are currently operating as branches in the EC to begin to plan how best to structure themselves to take advantage of the future single passport arrangements. In order to do this, they will need to incorporate a subsidiary in a suitable Member State, which will then become the authorizing home country for the purposes of the Investment Services Directive.

It is also worth bearing in mind that the single passport entitles an investment firm to establish a branch or branches in other member states (or to provide investment services there) but not to set up another subsidiary. The establishment of a subsidiary will still require approval by the Member State in which it is formed. The exception to this rule is expected to be where it is mandatory in the host country to be a corporate member of a local securities exchange, in which case home country authorization will permit the establishment of a subsidiary for this purpose in the host country.

Some non-EC investment firms may decide that the establishment of branches in other Member States does not provide the best answer to their business expansion needs and therefore will choose not to exercise the single passport option when it becomes available in January 1993. Equally, others may not wish to wait this long before beginning to expand within the EC. Apart from seeking, with host country approval, to set up subsidiaries, they may produce a noticeable increase in the number of share-exchanges, business alliances, or attempted acquisitions.

The Investment Services proposal was substantially amended in January 1990 to align it more closely to the banking directive. Originally scheduled to be adopted in 1989, the directive is considerably behind schedule and has some way to go to catch up with the banking directive. The aim is for both the second banking and the investment services directives to be in force by January 1, 1993, together with the supporting directives setting out the capital adequacy requirements of banks and nonbank investment firms and the setting of the capital adequacy directive for investment services has only now been tabled although the own funds and solvency ratios directives have already been adopted. There is a risk, therefore, that the banking directive could be implemented ahead of the directive on investment services.

This problem of timing of the directives could have important implications for nonbanking investment firms, which would face the prospect of being placed at a competitive disadvantage if banks were granted the freedom to conduct securities business EC-wide while they were still awaiting their EC-license for investment services. However, given that the two directives bear close resemblances in many respects, it is to be hoped that passage of the Investment Services Directive through the EC legislative machinery will proceed at a faster pace.

PROPOSED CAPITAL ADEQUACY DIRECTIVE

The long-awaited proposal for a directive that would set out the capital adequacy requirements for nonbank investment firms was finally announced in Brussels on April 24, 1990. Even before the official text of the proposal had been agreed upon (after several radically different versions of working papers were circulated informally and five drafts prepared), the directive has already been the subject of much debate. The UK securities industry, in particular, expressed fears that EC firms will be subjected to heavier capital requirements than their competitors from outside the EC. The industry has been anxious to prevent rules that could substantially increase costs or even force a number of firms out of business and to ensure that the directive differentiates among the different types of investment risks. There was also concern that securities firms could be placed at a competitive disadvantage compared to banks. Details of the contents of the proposal arrived as this book was going to print and appear on page xiii of the front matter.

PUBLIC OFFER PROSPECTUSES DIRECTIVE

This directive, adopted on April 17, 1989, lays down common requirements for the preparation, scrutiny, and distribution of prospectuses for first issues of securities to the public. The directive's overall objective is to ensure that prospective investors in all 12 Member States are provided with a common level of information which permits them to make a well-informed assessment of the risks involved when making investment decisions. This should increase investor confidence and thus encourage investment across EC frontiers.

The directive stipulates that prospectuses will have to be published when transferable securities are offered to the public for the first time, in one or more Member States. The directive's disclosure requirements for the contents of prospectuses are aimed at securing a minimum degree of protection for investors throughout the EC. The intent is to complement the existing 1980 Listing Particulars Directive 80/390, already referred to on page 128, which coordinates the information to be published when securities are admitted to stock exchange listing. Public offer prospectuses which are to be the subject of an application for official listing will have to comply with the rules concerning prospectuses stated in the 1980 Listing Particulars Directive.

Less onerous information requirements will, however, be applied to offers that do not relate to an application for official stock-exchange listing. In this case the prospectus must contain the information necessary to enable investors to make an informed assessment of the assets and liabilities, general financial position, profits and losses, and prospects of the issuer, and the rights attached to the securities.

The competent authority in the issuer's country of origin (where it has its registered office) will be responsible for checking that prospectuses are drawn up in accordance with the provisions of the directive.

Mutual Recognition

The directive introduces the principle of mutual recognition: a single public offers prospectus approved by the authorities of one Member State can be used for public offers of the same securities made simultaneously in other Member States. A prospectus would thus be recognized as complying with the laws of the other Member States without being subject to any additional form of approval or to a requirement to include any further information.

Member States will, however, be entitled to impose an obligation to include in the prospectus information relating specifically to the market of the country where the public offer is made. This could include information on the income tax system, the financial organizations retained to act as paying agents for the issuer, and the way in which notices to investors are published.

Among the types of offer excluded from the scope of the directive are Euro-securities, which are not the subject of a generalized advertising or canvassing campaign. Euro-securities are defined as transferable securities which are offered on a significant scale, are underwritten and distributed by a syndicate, at least two of whose members have their registered offices in different Member States, and can only be obtained through a credit or other financial institution.

This exemption for Euro-securities was introduced in response to the fears of Britain and Luxembourg that over-regulation might drive the high-volume Euro-securities business out of the EC to Switzerland and offshore centers. Both countries argued that there are few small Eurobond investors requiring protection and stressed that having to comply with the regulations contained in the directive would have a highly detrimental effect on the fast moving Eurobond market, in which new issues often have to be distributed within a single day.

The directive will not apply to the following types of offer:

- Offers to persons in the context of their trades, professions, or occupations; and/or
- Offers to a restricted circle of persons; and/or
- Offers where the selling price of all the securities offered does not exceed 40,000 ECU, or where the securities can be acquired only for a minimum investment of at least 40,000 ECU per investor.

Apart from Euro-securities, certain other types of transferable securities will also be excluded:

- Securities offered in individual denominations of at least 40,000 ECU
- Units issued by collective investment undertakings (UCITS) other than the closed-end type
- Securities issued by Member States or their regional or local authorities
- Securities offered in connection with a takeover bid or merger

- Shares allotted to shareholders free of charge
- Shares offered to or for the benefit of employees
- Shares resulting from the conversion of debt securities
- Shares issued by nonprofit bodies, building societies, or industrial and provident societies

The directive also includes provisions concerning reciprocal arrangements with non-EC countries. The principle of mutual recognition of prospectuses can thus be extended to include prospectuses issued by third-country firms by means of reciprocal agreements to be concluded between the EC and the countries concerned. Public offer prospectuses drawn up and scrutinized in accordance with the rules of a non-EC country may be recognized as meeting the reciprocity requirements of the directive, provided that the rules concerned give investors protection equivalent to that provided by the directive and even if the rules are different.

PUBLIC OFFER PROSPECTUSES FOR USE AS LISTING PARTICULARS

In April 1990 the European Commission adopted a new directive that will amend the 1987 Listing Particulars Directive. Now public offer prospectuses that meet the requirements of the Public Offer Prospectuses Directive and become approved in one Member State will be mutually recognized for use as listing particulars, to gain admission to official stock exchange listing anywhere in the EC. An approved prospectus will thus automatically be recognized by the authorities of the other Member States where application for official listing is made, without being subject to any form of approval or being required to furnish any additional information in the prospectus.

This new directive is considered necessary because the 1987 Directive limits the scope of mutual recognition of public offer prospectuses as listing particulars to offers where listing is requested in at least two Member States, one of which is involved in the public offer. The amendment is therefore aimed at extending mutual recognition to include cases where admission is requested in only one Member State, irrespective of whether it is involved in the public offer.

The intention was for the new directive to be adopted by the end of 1989, and to be implemented into national legislation by January 1, 1990, in order to coincide with the entry into force of the 1987 Listing Particulars Directive due on that date. A common position was agreed on November 13, 1989, and the proposal received the final approval of the European Parliament on January 17, 1990, subject to minor amendments. These were incorporated in the final directive adopted on April 24, 1990.

INSIDER TRADING DIRECTIVE

A directive that was not originally foreseen in the 1985 White Paper was adopted on November 13, 1989, to outlaw insider trading throughout the EC. It introduces minimum EC-wide rules for insider trading, defines the terms "inside information" and "insider," and provides for close cooperation and exchanges of information among the appropriate supervisory authorities in each Member State. Member States are required to introduce the new legislation by June 1, 1992—in time to combat any illegal dealing following the liberalization of capital movements.

The directive aims to ensure that investors are placed on an equal footing by affording them adequate protection against the improper use of inside information. The new rules are therefore intended to limit the scope for deriving unfair advantage from the liberalization of capital movements.

When the directive was first drafted, in response to several major insider trading scandals, most Member States had no national rules or regulations prohibiting insider trading and the rules that did exist differed significantly from one Member State to another. Currently eight of the 12 Member States now have their own national rules, although these are very different.

The directive draws a distinction between two categories of insider. "Primary insiders" are those who have access to inside information through their employment, profession, or duties, or as shareholders, or through membership of the administrative, management, or supervisory units of the issuer. "Secondary insiders" are those who have knowingly obtained inside information from a primary insider.

Inside information is defined as:

- Information that has not been made public
- Information of a precise nature (a simple rumor would not be considered inside information)
- Information that relates to one or more issuers of transferable securities (e.g., concerning an increase in profits or a takeover bid) or to one or more transferable securities (information likely to influence the market)
- Information that, if it were made public, would be likely to have a significant effect on the prices of the securities of a company

The directive obliges the Member States to forbid both the improper use of this information by the insiders, either for their own benefit or others', and the communication of this information to another person:

- Primary insiders would be prohibited from taking advantage of such information, in full knowledge of the facts, to buy or sell, either directly or indirectly, securities of the issuer to which that information relates.

- Insiders who have acquired inside information would be prohibited from disclosing it to a third party unless such disclosure were made in the normal course of their duties.
- "Tipping" (using the information to recommend that a third party buy or sell securities) would be forbidden.

Secondary insiders would be prohibited from knowingly taking similar advantage of inside information disclosed to them by primary insiders, from divulging the information to third parties, and from tipping.

An addition to the directive allows exemptions to be made in special cases so that bona fide professionals with legitimate reasons for dealing are not charged with or found guilty of insider dealing. These exemptions include stockbrokers and privatizations.

Each Member State will be required to designate the authority or authorities to be responsible for monitoring compliance with the directive and to ensure that these authorities possess sufficiently wide supervisory and investigative powers where offenses are committed.

The directive also imposes an obligation on Member States to introduce sufficiently deterrent penalties, to ensure compliance. It does not, however, provide for harmonized legal sanctions but leaves it up to the individual Member States to determine the penalties for infringement under national law. Member States will have the option of imposing more stringent rules than those laid down in the directive, provided that they are nondiscriminatory.

The directive also sets out rules providing for close cooperation and exchange of information among the Member States' supervisory authorities, to assist in the pursuit of offenders. To ensure that information communicated in this way remains confidential, employees of such authorities would be bound to respect professional secrecy rules.

The provisions on information exchange have proved to be controversial. A Member State will be required to supply all the information needed by another Member State in its insider trading investigations, even if the quantity of information is more than the cooperating Member State would itself be allowed, under its national legislation, to request of another EC authority. Refusal to supply information will only be justifiable where communication of the information might adversely affect the sovereignty of the state or where judicial proceedings have already been initiated or a final judgment has been passed on the same case.

Another area of dispute concerns the identification of the location where an offense is deemed to have occurred. It has now been agreed that this shall be determined by the country in which the illegal transaction has been effected and not by the nationality of the offender or the company concerned. The national authorities of the relevant country will thus be responsible for following up the offense.

The Directive also contains provisions allowing the EC to conclude agreements with non-EC countries on the matters regulated by the directive.

MAJOR SHAREHOLDINGS DIRECTIVE

Adopted on December 12, 1988, this directive on major transfers of share ownership sets out detailed rules on the information that must be published when a major holding in a listed company is acquired or disposed of. Member States are required to take the necessary steps to comply with the directive by January 1, 1991.

Known as the "antiraider" directive, its purpose is to ensure that investors and the public at large will be informed of major shareholdings and of changes affecting voting rights, above certain thresholds, in EC-listed companies.

As with other proposals in the securities sector, it is intended to reinforce at the multinational EC level the policy of providing adequate investment information in order to improve investors' protection, increase investors' confidence in securities markets, and ensure that securities markets function effectively. By establishing equivalent levels of protection throughout the EC, the directive aims to facilitate greater interpenetration of the Member States' transferable securities markets and so contribute toward the creation of a true European capital market.

The European Commission recognizes that listed companies are unable to notify the public of changes in major shareholdings unless they have first been informed of such changes by the relevant shareholders. Most Member States do not impose such disclosure requirements on shareholders; where such obligations exist the methods of application differ considerably.

Although the 1979 Admissions Directive, which regulates conditions for admission to a stock exchange, already obliges companies to inform the public of major changes in share ownership, in practice companies often do not know themselves when such changes have taken place.

The directive aims to fill the gaps in existing legislation and to harmonize rules in this field by obliging buyers and sellers of significant blocks of shares (above certain thresholds affecting voting rights) to notify the company within seven days. Important changes will result in those countries where no rules exist to force parties acquiring shares to reveal their identity.

Significant holdings in a company are defined as 10, 20, 33 1/3, 50, and 66 2/3 percent. If a change in ownership of shares causes a buyer's or seller's shareholding in a listed company to exceed, or fall below, one of these thresholds, the buyer or seller will have to inform the company and the competent authorities within 7 days. These thresholds are the same as those used in existing EC Company Law Directives as measures of significant influence.

The directive also stipulates that at the first general meeting of a company held more than three months after the directive has been implemented into national law, all shareholders in possession of 10 percent or more of voting rights must make a declaration of their holdings to the company and the competent authorities, specifying the proportion of voting rights actually held.

The directive reinforces the companies' obligation to inform the public if they themselves become aware of a significant transfer of share ownership. This is especially important in the case of buyers or sellers of shares located in non-EC countries who would not be subject to the rules of the directive. The company must inform the public of any changes in the structure of the major holdings in its capital, revealed in lists of shareholders and breakdowns of holdings, as soon as such changes come to its notice.

A company that has received a declaration must in turn disclose it to the public in each of the Member States where its shares are officially listed on a stock exchange, as soon as possible but not more than nine days after the declaration has been received. The information must be published in one or more newspapers distributed widely in the Member State concerned. Member States may provide for the disclosure to the public to be made by the competent authorities of the Member State concerned or by the companies themselves.

The directive allows for exemptions so that Member States can apply one threshold of 25 percent, instead of the 20 and 33 1/3 percent thresholds, and a 75 percent threshold instead of the 66 2/3 percent threshold. Member States may impose more stringent requirements than those contained in the directive.

The directive is regarded as particularly important in light of anticipated restructuring, in the race to create a single market by 1992.

PROPOSAL TO ABOLISH ALL TAXES ON SECURITIES TRANSACTIONS

On April 2, 1976, the European Commission initially put forward a proposal for a directive to harmonize indirect taxes on transactions in securities. The aim was to remove distortions in competition caused by the highly divergent rates of taxation on transactions in securities in the EC. These ranged (in July 1987) from the application of no such taxes in Luxembourg, Portugal, and Greece to the relatively high rates of 10 percent in Ireland and Denmark, 5 percent in the UK, 3.5 percent in Belgium, and a rate of around 1–2 percent in the other Member States.

However, harmonization in this area has proved to be practically impossible because of the vast differences in the method of collection and numerous complex technical problems. As a result no agreement was reached on the proposal.

With the adoption of the capital movements directive in 1986, the Commission decided to produce a revised proposal to abolish these taxes. This latter Directive, effective as of February 28, 1987, extended the obligation to liberalize capital movements to include all operations involving the acquisition of securities as well as operations involving the admission to the capital market of negotiable securities plus those which are in the process of being introduced onto a stock exchange.

Little progress has been made, however, on the new proposal, which set January 1, 1990, as the target date for the abolition of taxes on securities. The aims were to allow firms unhindered access to the capital markets and financial centers of the EC, and to eliminate distortions in capital movements and competition arising from double taxation, and discrimination incompatible with the internal market.

The proposal included provisions designed to protect the effects of the abolition of these taxes from being nullified by the introduction of other taxes having the same base, while at the same time permitting Member States to impose taxes and duties which would not hamper free circulation of capital.

The proposal would have involved changes for the majority of Member States since all, with the exception of Luxembourg, Greece, and Portugal, levy indirect taxes on share transactions. The UK in particular earns heavy revenue from such transactions.

EUROPEAN SECURITIES MARKET

The 1985 White Paper mentioned initiatives being taken toward the creation of a European securities market system based on electronic interlinking of EC stock exchanges, so that clients' orders could be executed on the stock exchange market offering the most advantageous terms. Initial steps have been taken to link together stock exchanges in different Member States within the framework of the Interbourse Data Information Exchange System (IDIS).

A parallel initiative underway is the Pipe, an integrated network linking stock exchanges throughout the EC. The system, which is still in the early stages, is being developed among the EC stock exchanges themselves and will allow investors access to stock exchange information from EC members.

8

Liberalization of Capital Movements

In addition to the measures described in the preceding chapters for the harmonization of national supervisory rules in financial services, the following are considered by the European Commission as essential preconditions for the creation of a European financial area:

1. Strengthening of the European Monetary System
2. Measures to combat tax evasion
3. Implementation of the full liberalization of capital movements

Alongside the free movement of goods, services, and persons, the free movement of capital within the EC is one of the "four freedoms" dating back to the treaty establishing the EC. Article 67 of the Treaty of Rome calls for the Member States "to progressively abolish between themselves all restrictions on the movement of capital. . . ."

The Commission views the free movement of capital as being necessary for the proper functioning of the internal market and a fundamental element for the realization of a financial area without frontiers, in which there is complete freedom for financial institutions to offer their services to savers and investors throughout the EC either by establishing branches or through the provision of financial services on a cross-border basis.

Businesses and individual consumers should have access to the widest possible range of efficient financial services available and should be permitted to open bank accounts, invest their savings, and lend or borrow money in any of the twelve Member States.

In its 1985 White Paper, the Commission announced a two-stage program for completing the liberalization of capital movements. The first was completed with the adoption of the 1986 capital movements directive, which amended the first Council directive (1960) for the implementation of Article 67 of the treaty. Its purpose was to liberalize those capital operations which were essential for the proper functioning of a single market and for the interlinking of financial markets.

The list of liberalized transactions was extended to include long-term commercial credits, transactions in securities not traded on a stock exchange (shares, bonds, unit trusts), the admission of a company's securities to the capital market of another Member State, and so forth.

The second stage, presented in 1987, aims to complete the process of liberalization so that what is known as the "European financial area" will become a reality. Once this second stage is accomplished, EC nationals will have free access to the financial systems of other EC countries and will be able to carry out any investment, borrowing, or lending activities.

Three proposals for legislation to complete the full liberalization of capital movements by 1992 were unanimously adopted by the Member States in June 1988 and are due to enter into force by June 1990, with a transitional period for Ireland, Greece, Spain, and Portugal.

DIRECTIVE ON THE FULL LIBERALIZATION OF CAPITAL MOVEMENTS

The purpose of this directive, based on Article 67 of the EC Treaty, is to remove all existing restrictions on exchange controls and extend liberalization to the remaining capital movements—investments in short-term securities, current and deposit accounts, and financial loans and credits. The directive states that: "Member States shall abolish restrictions on movements of capital taking place between persons resident in Member States . . . ."

The countries that will be most directly affected are France, Denmark, Italy, Ireland, Spain, Portugal, and Greece; restrictions have already been abolished in the other Member States. The UK, West Germany, and the Netherlands have already phased out exchange controls. In Denmark, however, residents are still required to obtain authorization in order to open bank accounts abroad. France and Italy have already taken steps to ease exchange controls in advance of the July 1, 1990, deadline. France decided to deregulate capital flows from January 1, 1990, and Italy has partly lifted exchange controls to allow residents to acquire foreign securities. In March 1990, Belgium and Luxembourg abolished their dual exchange system, viewed by the Commission as being incompatible with the EMS, in the interests of effective implementation of the Directive.

Member States will be allowed to impose restrictions on the free movement of capital in certain specific circumstances. For instance, in the interests of consumer protection, national monetary authorities would still be entitled to lay down prudential rules aimed at ensuring that financial institutions are adequately covered against exchange and investment risks.

Safeguard Clause

As a protective measure, the directive contains a special safeguard clause authorizing Member States to take any necessary safeguard measures in the event of serious tension or upset of monetary markets. Member States may reintroduce temporary controls on short-term capital movements if they present a risk of seriously disrupting a member country's monetary or exchange rate policy. The measures would be limited to a maximum of six months and they could apply only to short-term operations (especially current account or deposit operations on the money market).

A Member State wishing to invoke the safeguard clause would first have to notify and obtain authorization from the European Commission, which would stipulate the conditions and terms. However, in an emergency situation the country concerned could take the necessary steps without waiting for the Commission's response, as long as it informed the Commission and the other Member States of the actions taken.

Transitional Period

The Commission recognizes that the liberalization of capital movements will pose special problems for those Member States with balance-of-payments difficulties or high levels of external indebtedness, and could hinder their efforts to adapt to the requirements of an integrated financial services market.

Spain, Ireland, Greece, and Portugal have thus been granted extra time to comply with the directive and may continue to impose certain restrictions until the end of 1992.

Greece and Portugal will be able to extend this derogation for another three years.

Protective Measures vis-à-vis *Non-EC Countries*

The directive also introduces an amendment to the 1972 directive on the regulation of international capital flows. Member States must aim to achieve the same degree of liberalization of capital movements for operations with countries outside the Community: "In their treatment of transfers in respect of movements of capital to or from third countries, the Member States shall endeavour to attain the same degree of liberalization as that which applies to operations with residents of other Member States. . . ." The Commission should be notified of any such transactions with third countries and in certain circumstances would be able to make recommendations to the Member States.

The directive also provides for joint EC action in the event of large capital flows. Where large-scale, short-term capital movements to or from third countries seriously disturb the domestic or external monetary or financial situation of the Member States, or cause serious strain in exchange relations within the EC or between the EC and outside countries, Member States must consult each other on any proposed remedial measures.

REGULATION TO CREATE A MEDIUM-TERM FINANCIAL SUPPORT INSTRUMENT

This Regulation established a single instrument to provide medium-term financial support (MTFS) by combining the existing EC loan and medium-term financial assistance mechanisms; the MTFS instrument became the primary instrument for medium-term aid. It can assist Member States that experience particular problems in participating in the process of attaining full liberalization of capital movements, and can offer the possibility of temporary assistance to countries with balance-of-payments difficulties. Decisions relating to the granting of loans to Member States would have to be taken by the Council on the basis of qualified majority voting. Financial support would be available up to a maximum of 16 million ECU.

9

Complementary Supporting Measures: Company Law and Tax Approximation

The many variations in the tax, company law, and accounting provisions of the different Member States represent a major barrier to the creation of a genuinely integrated market and can result in distortions of competition. A firm from one Member State could, for instance, find itself at a significant disadvantage in relation to a competitor from another Member State because of having to comply with more onerous regulatory requirements. Different tax regimes and rates may distort investment decisions, since tax considerations frequently have a key role in determining where a business may decide to invest; and differing accounting and disclosure rules make it difficult to compare the financial performance of companies from the Member States.

The European Commission has put forward a comprehensive range of proposals aimed at eliminating these anomalies and ensuring a common level of protection and high standards of disclosure and information for investors and shareholders throughout the EC. The proposals are designed to remove the legal, fiscal, and administrative obstacles to greater cross-border cooperation, and to create a favorable business environment for companies to operate in the enlarged European market.

To this end, the Commission has embarked on a comprehensive program to harmonize national company laws with the objective of establishing a uniform legal framework for EC companies. Prior to the launch of the single market program, a substantial framework of EC company law had already been put in place. Legislation, principally concerned with public limited companies, has been adopted governing such matters as disclosure and capital requirements, company accounts and consolidated accounts, formation of a company, the qualifications of auditors, legal mergers and divisions. Two further directives adopted at the end of December 1989 are the Eleventh Directive to dispense branches of companies based in other EC countries from publishing separate accounts and the Twelfth Directive to allow the formation of single-member companies.

The important directives in this area are the fourth and seventh company law directives, which deal respectively with the content, presentation, and publication of company accounts and the preparation of consolidated accounts for groups of companies.

Despite this progress a large number of company law measures remain to be adopted; some of them were first tabled as long as 20 years ago. Two key proposals still outstanding are the controversial draft fifth company law directive, covering the structure and management of public limited companies, and the regulation to create a European Company Statute. The former introduces a mandatory system of employee participation in company decision making and a dual board system (management and supervisory) organized either on the German two-tier or the UK one-tier system. The Company Statute would provide an optional form of European company structure, independent of individual national laws, so as to allow transnational companies to operate more easily across the EC without the need to be established in different Member States. Tax advantages would allow losses suffered in one Member State to be offset against profits in another. As with the fifth directive, the fiercely debated provisions for worker participation and information and consultation rights have contributed to the proposal's being stalled for many years.

Other proposals in the company law harmonization program include the draft tenth directive on cross-border mergers, and the proposal, still to be published, for a ninth directive governing the relationship between parent companies and their subsidiaries, and a further directive to harmonize procedures for the voluntary winding-up and liquidation of companies.

TAKEOVERS PROPOSAL

Takeovers are not yet covered in the company law program. With the gradual freeing of capital movements and the advent of a single market, takeover activity in the EC is growing; with this in mind the European Commission presented, at the end of 1988, proposals for a new key company law directive. If adopted, this proposed thirteenth company law directive will establish a framework of minimum rules governing the conduct of takeover bids. Its aim is to facilitate constructive takeovers, while preventing speculative bids and ensuring proper disclosure and transparency so as to afford shareholders and other interested parties equivalent standards of protection in all Member States.

Current practices and experience relating to takeovers vary significantly among the different Member States. Some have already introduced legislation dealing with takeover bids (Spain, France, and Portugal) and others have voluntary codes of practice (Germany, Italy, Netherlands, UK, and Ireland). In countries such as Denmark and Greece, however, takeover bids are practically unknown and as yet no such rules exist. The main features of the proposed directive are described in the following sections.

Obligation to Make a Bid

No partial bids will be permitted: to prevent purely speculative bids the directive requires the bidder to bid for the whole company, not just part of it. In special cases the supervisory authority will be able to grant exemptions to this rule.

Anyone acquiring a certain percentage of the shares will be obliged to launch a formal takeover bid so that all shareholders will be able to benefit equally from the higher price offered by the bidder in order to acquire a block of shares. Member States will have to fix a threshold no higher than one-third of total shares. Exemptions will, however, be allowed for smaller companies and those not quoted on a stock exchange.

Offer Prospectuses

The directive establishes the fundamental principle of equality of treatment of those to whom a takeover is addressed. To ensure that shareholders and other interested parties are properly informed of what is going on during a takeover bid, it sets out detailed rules on the information that must be provided to shareholders and employees and imposes on the bidder the obligation to issue an offer prospectus outlining his or her intentions. This prospectus will have to include details of the bidder's plans for the use to be made of the company's assets, the company's future activities, the continued employment of the staff, and the level of future debts. The intention is to help discourage leveraged buyouts.

In a report setting out the arguments for and against acceptance of the bid, full information will have to be provided to shareholders and employees' representatives concerning the views of the directors of the target company, the rules to apply if a competing bid is made, the intentions of the bidder, and the response of the target company to the offer.

Defensive Measures

The directive includes rules prohibiting certain kinds of defensive ("poison-pill") measures taken by managements after a bid is announced. The directive's aim is to prevent managements from acting in their own self-interest rather than for the wider interests of the company and its shareholders. Once a management has received official notification of a bid and while the offer is still open, the management will be prohibited from taking action to impede the bid, such as issuing any shares, or engaging in operations of an exceptional nature, such as increasing capital or selling assets without first being authorized to do so through a general meeting of the shareholders. This latter condition has aroused some criticism on the grounds that it could lead to responses to bids being greatly protracted.

Compliance

To ensure compliance with the directive, Member States will be required to appoint a supervisory authority that will have the power to police effectively the rules of the directive. The supervisory authority will be able to forbid the publication of an incomplete prospectus or to request the bidder to resubmit a revised offer prospectus. The directive also sets out a rule for determining which supervisory authority will be responsible when bids are launched simultaneously in more than one Member State. Responsibility will rest with the authority in the country where the target company has its registered office and in such cases mutual recognition of offer prospectuses will apply.

Reciprocity

There is no reciprocity clause relating to takeovers from non-EC countries in the proposed directive, but Member States will still be able to impose any national reciprocity rules concerning takeover bids from third countries.

The proposal states that the directive "does not until subsequent coordination affect the capacity of Member States to forbid a takeover bid where the offeror is either a national or a company from a third country, especially when community nationals and companies do not benefit from reciprocal treatment for acquiring shares by means of a takeover bid in a company governed from that third country."

The EC intends to open negotiations on the question of reciprocity with other countries. The Commission is currently preparing a revised proposal in response to amendments proposed by the European Parliament in its opinion delivered on January 16, 1990. These call for greater influence and protection to employees of the target company during the period of a takeover and the restriction of the directive to listed companies while allowing Member States the possibility of extending it to cover unlisted companies as well. In addition to the proposed directive the Commission is presently conducting a study of obstacles to takeovers in the EC, and is expected to submit proposals early in 1990 for legislation to address these problems, probably in a new and separate directive. (A significant development also worth noting here was the adoption by the Council on December 21, 1989, of a regulation concerning the control of mergers and acquisitions. The regulation, which enters into force in September 1990, will give the European Commission powers to investigate large cross-border mergers of a Community dimension—above certain defined thresholds.)

TAXATION

Once the full liberalization of capital movements comes into effect, tax considerations could have an increasingly influential effect on capital flows. The dismantling of barriers will increase the significance of these tax considerations, since in theory it will be easier to establish in one Member State and sell to another.

In the capital movements directive, a provision stated that the Commission would undertake to produce proposals aimed at reducing the risks of tax distortions and evasion after the directive comes into force. The Commission is thus proposing measures to ensure that substantial differences in matters of taxation do not cause distortions that might affect the functioning of the capital market.

Taxation proposals have, however, so far proved to be particularly problematic since all taxation measures must be adopted unanimously by the Council. Proposals to harmonize the direct tax systems of the Member States date as far back as 1969 but so far no directives in this field have yet been adopted although work is currently continuing on some of them and others have been resuscitated.

Discriminatory Tax Incentives

Tax provisions that encourage the purchase of domestic securities exist in many EC countries. The European Commission is proposing a gradual elimination of these discriminatory measures and the distortions they create.

Company Taxation

Investment decisions and competition are also frequently distorted by significant differences in company taxation among the Member States. Some approximation of company taxation is therefore considered necessary so that the full benefits of the liberalization of capital movements may be realized.

To eliminate these distortions, the Commission is offering a series of proposals for harmonizing the tax systems, tax bases, and tax rates in the Member States and for strengthening the procedures for cooperation among national tax authorities. These proposed taxation measures include a package of three draft directives, two of which date back to 1969:

1. A proposal for a common system of taxation applicable to parent companies and their subsidiaries
2. A proposal for a common system of taxation of mergers, divisions, and so on, to remove the obstacles to intra-EC cooperation
3. A proposal for an arbitration procedure directed toward the elimination of double taxation

These were resurrected at an ECOFIN meeting in June 1989 but again little headway was made in breaching the 20-year impasse. In an effort to break the deadlock on tax proposals, Christiane Scrivener, the European Commissioner responsible for taxation, recently put forward the suggestion that the forthcoming conference on the revision of the EC Treaty should also look at the possibility of making tax proposals the subject of majority voting instead of requiring unanimity as at present.

On April 18, 1990, the Commission adopted a communication setting out a new approach to company taxation. Instead of attempting, as previously, to harmonize company taxation schemes along the lines of proposals submitted in 1975, the new strategy will be based on mutual recognition and coordination between the Member States. A committee of experts will also be nominated to study the extent to which disparities in company taxation distort investment decisions and competition in the single market. In addition to the three existing proposals listed above, the Commission intends to propose two further measures. The first would allow companies to offset losses of subsidiaries in one country against profits in another. The second would deal with interest and royalty payments within company groups.

Tax Evasion

The European Commission is considering two types of measures to reduce the increased risks of tax evasion likely to result from investors having greater ease in collecting income outside their country of residence. The first would introduce a uniform withholding tax, at source, applicable to all EC residents on interest income. The second would require banks to disclose to tax authorities the details of interest income received by EC residents. This measure would ensure that taxpayers pay all the tax due to their tax authorities, but would entail the abolition of banking secrecy in those Member States where it is applied. Such a system of disclosure already exists in Denmark and the Netherlands.

The fear has been expressed, by France and some other Member States, that the removal of all restrictions on capital movements could cause a migration of capital and savings to countries with more flexible tax systems or to tax havens outside the EC. When investors have the freedom to choose an investment in any Member State, regardless of their place of residence, the risk of their income not being declared will increase.

Both alternatives pose particular problems. Certain Member States would be extremely reluctant to agree to either. The question also arises: Will the imposition of measures designed to curb tax evasion have the effect of driving savings outside the EC instead?

WITHHOLDING TAX PROPOSAL

On February 10, 1989, the Commission proposed the introduction of a minimum 15 percent withholding tax on interest received by EC residents. This tax is aimed at preventing capital from flowing toward countries with less onerous taxation regimes, such as the UK and Luxembourg, and offsetting the risks of tax evasion once the planned removal of all remaining EC capital controls comes into effect in July 1990.

The new tax, which introduces the concept of "Community resident," would apply to everyone resident in the EC for tax purposes. Several Member States, including the UK, Ireland, and Luxembourg, impose no such withholding tax on income of nonresidents and those taxes that do exist vary substantially from one Member State to another (see Table 9–1). The 15 percent rate was selected as representing the average in the EC, where rates vary from 0 to 35 percent.

The withholding tax proposal has aroused considerable controversy. Belgium, France, and Italy, for whom taxation of savings represents a large source of revenue, view the introduction of a withholding tax as essential, to counter the risk of distortions in competition once financial frontiers are dismantled. Without it, they claim, savings will be diverted to countries like Luxembourg, where more favorable tax regimes do not levy withholding taxes.

Not surprisingly, Luxembourg is strongly opposed to the introduction of the withholding tax and would be unwilling to relinquish its favorable tax system. Likewise, the UK believes there is no need for a withholding tax, preferring instead to leave it to market forces to iron out the discrepancies.

Member States with low tax rates—again, Luxembourg and the UK—claim that the 15 percent rate is too high and may provoke a flight of capital to non-EC countries like Switzerland, where withholding taxes are not levied. Another worry is that European financial centers could be placed at a competitive disadvantage as a result of the proposed tax, because of the prospect of European savings going elsewhere to evade the tax.

In an effort to avoid driving savings outside the EC for tax reasons and to preserve the competitiveness of EC financial centers, the proposal allows some exemptions. It would, for instance, not apply to: investors from outside the EC, small savings schemes that are not subject to national income tax, Eurobonds, or share dividends. Member States that have a system of automatic disclosure by banks to the tax authorities, such as France, would also be exempt from the obligation to apply withholding tax to interest paid to their residents. [At the same time as the withholding tax proposal, the European Commission proposed a second directive, to amend an earlier (1977) directive on mutual assistance among national tax authorities. Aimed at strengthening cooperation among these authorities, the directive would remove the administrative barriers that impede exchange of information and frustrate tax enquiries among EC countries in cases where fraud is suspected. Banking secrecy laws would not be affected.]

The proposed withholding tax has suffered a considerable setback since Germany's decision to abolish its own 10 percent withholding tax at source only introduced in January 1989. Germany experienced substantial outflows of capital when it announced the imposition of the tax, and has now sided with the

Table 9–1
Taxation of Interest on Capital
Position as of January 1, 1989

	Residents	*Nonresidents*	*Residents*	*Nonresidents*
	Withholding Tax on Interest on Bonds (Subject to the Provisions of Double Taxation Conventions)		*Withholding Tax on Interest on Bank and Savings Accounts (Subject to the Provisions of Double Taxation Conventions)*	
Luxembourg	—	—	—	—
Netherlands	Automatic communication from banks to administration	—	Automatic communication from banks to administration	—
Portugal	25%	25%	20%	20%
Belgium	25%	—	25%	—
Denmark	Automatic communication from banks to administration	—	—	—
France	Automatic communication from banks to tax administration or different rates discharging of debt	0%	Automatic communication from banks to tax administration or different rates discharging of debt	
Ireland	35% (exceptions)	35% (exceptions)	35%	0%

Spain	20% (exceptions)	20% (exceptions)	20%	20%
United Kingdom	25% (exceptions)	25% (exceptions)	25% residents	0%
Greece	Companies: with permanent establishment, 25% without permanent establishment, 49% Persons: at progressive rates of income tax; 0% public loans and bonds of corporations engaged in industrial activities	Companies: with permanent establishment, 25% without permanent establishment, 49% Persons: at progressive rates of income tax; 0% public loans and bonds of corporations engaged in industrial activities	Companies: with permanent establishment, 25% without permanent establishment, 49%	Companies: with permanent establishment, 25% without permanent establishment, 49%
Germany	10%	10%	10%	10%
Italy	12.5% discharging of debt (no choice for the beneficiary)	12.5% discharging of debt (no choice for the beneficiary)	30%	30%

Source: Official Journal of the European Communities, August 28, 1989.

UK and Luxembourg in firmly opposing the tax. The prospect of the proposal's ever being adopted now seems increasingly remote, although it has not officially been withdrawn.

The Commission has turned its attention toward examining other means of reinforcing cooperation among national tax authorities and introducing greater flexibility in bank secrecy laws. In July 1989, it drew up new guidelines for combating tax evasion through strengthening of fiscal cooperation among national tax administrations. These guidelines included encouraging taxpayers to declare their earnings from investments and savings; obliging EC residents to make declarations when exporting a large amount of capital; and reinforcing and extending the proposal to revise the 1977 directive on exchange of information among tax authorities to include gift taxes and estate duties within its scope. With the aim of strengthening cooperation with tax authorities outside the EC, the Commission also proposed renewing bilateral talks on fiscal cooperation with the US, Japan, and member countries of EFTA, and recommended that all EC Member States should ratify the 1959 Council of Europe Convention on judicial cooperation and the protocol on tax offenses.

On December 18, 1989, ECOFIN reached partial agreement on a compromise text, with 11 Member States in favor of measures to tighten up cooperation among tax authorities and with non-EC countries. Luxembourg was the only country to express opposition because of its reluctance to agree to any easing of banking secrecy laws.

REMOVING THE FISCAL BARRIERS

The European Commission's proposals for approximating value-added tax (VAT) rates and excise duties are likely to prove to be one of the most problematic areas of the internal market program for the Council to adopt.

All the Member States have now implemented the same system of VAT but there are still significant variations among Member States in the number and level of VAT rates. Differences in excise duties on oil products, alcoholic drinks, tobacco products, and so on, result in the distortion of competition and frontier controls (see Table 9–2).

In the view of the Commission, there cannot be a true single market without the total elimination of tax controls at frontiers. The complete abolition of intra-EC border checks would mean that shoppers in the EC could undertake cross-border shopping and move freely between high taxing countries and low taxing countries. They would be able to take advantage of the huge differentials in the wide-ranging VAT rates and excise duties which currently exist throughout the EC.

Table 9–2
Examples of Excise Duties in Member States (March 1985)

	ECU					
Member State	*20 Cigar-ettes*	*1 Litre of Beer*	*1 Litre of Wine*	*0.75 Litre of 40% Spirits*	*1 Litre of Premium Petrol*	*Revenue from These Excises in Percent of GDP*[1]
Belgium	0.73	0.13	0.33	3.78	0.25	2.29%
Denmark	1.96	0.65	1.35	9.58[2]	0.28	3.27
Germany	1.02	0.07	0.00	3.43	0.23	2.58
France	0.31	0.03	0.03	3.37	0.36	2.12
Greece	0.28	0.22	0.00	0.16	0.29	n.a
Ireland	1.14	1.14	2.74	7.84	0.36	7.63
Italy	0.57	0.18	0.00	0.75	0.49	2.72
Luxembourg	0.54	0.06	0.13	2.54	0.20	3.75
Netherlands	0.74	0.23	0.33	3.79	0.28	1.92
United Kingdom	1.25	0.70	1.60	7.70	0.29	4.35

Source: European Commission.

[1] 1982 figures.

[2] Estimated average.

The Commission has therefore produced a package of proposals directed principally at removing the need for fiscal controls and checks at borders. These proposals cover the rates of VAT and excise duties that Member States can levy and changes in the way these taxes are collected and enforced.

It was originally proposed that Member States should set VAT rates within two bands—a standard rate of between 14 and 20 percent and a reduced rate of between 4 and 9 percent for certain basic goods and services such as food, public transport, domestic energy, and books and newspapers. Excise duties would, however, be set uniformly throughout the EC; the levels proposed would generally reflect the average of Member States' existing duty rates, which currently vary enormously from one Member State to another.

The Commission would treat sales and purchases across intra-EC frontiers in exactly the same way as sales and purchases within a single Member State. Exporters would charge the usual positive VAT rate on sales (instead of using the current zero-rating system), for exports and for domestic transactions, and importers would reclaim it as input tax, just as they would for domestic purchases.

To deal with the redistribution of revenues, the Commission has proposed setting up a VAT clearing house to ensure that VAT collected in the exporting Member State and deducted in the importing state accrues to the revenue authorities of the latter, where final consumption takes place.

The tax rate proposals, which have attracted a great deal of controversy, would result in a significant reduction in indirect tax revenues for some Member States such as Denmark and the Republic of Ireland. Others, notably Spain and Portugal, would experience substantial increases through having to impose for the first time substantial levels of excise duty on alcoholic drinks and tobacco products.

A number of other issues have been raised, including the health consequences of changes in the taxation of alcoholic and tobacco products. Changes in tax rates and in the structure of duties are also likely to affect the pattern of consumer spending and demand in different sectors.

The prices of several products would also be affected. In Italy, for example, the price of petrol would fall significantly. The price of cigarettes would increase dramatically in Greece and Spain, whereas in Denmark it would drop significantly.

The UK and Ireland have been staunchly opposed to these proposals because most zero-rated goods, including basic commodities such as food and children's clothes, would no longer be exempt from VAT and would have to bear the reduced rate of 4 to 9 percent. Denmark, which has a much higher VAT rate than the other EC countries, is concerned that it will face a drastic reduction in tax revenue. France, on the other hand, has criticized the proposals on the grounds that the range of permitted tax rates is too wide and could lead to trade distortions that would benefit countries that apply lower rates.

Moreover, Member States disagree as to whether approximation is necessary at all. The UK is arguing that market forces should be left to bring about a convergence of the EC's widely differing VAT rates.

After much opposition to the original proposals, the Commission produced a new package and dropped some of the more controversial aspects contained in the original draft. The revised proposals would allow for:

- A transitional phase, to the end of 1992. During this period Member States would be required to take steps to bring their VAT rates nearer to those of the other Member States and to simplify fiscal checks at frontiers.
- A zero-rating option for some basic commodities that are not traded across borders; other essential items would be included under the 4–9 percent band. (The

UK would be able to continue to apply zero-rating to food and children's clothing.)

- A simple minimum rate, expected to be in the region of 15 percent, and no maximum upper limit, instead of the originally proposed upper band. Member States would have the option of setting any rate above the minimum level.
- A simplified version of the Commission's proposed VAT clearing house system.

The Commission has withdrawn its plans for a single rate of EC excise duty for tobacco, alcohol, and petrol. Its new guidelines set recommended minimum target rates which Member States must reach. The time period is unspecified but the aim is for these minimum rates to be applied from January 1, 1993 on.

At a meeting of ECOFIN on November 13, 1989, approval was given to a formula that will allow zero-rated exports to continue and VAT and excise duties to be levied in the country of consumption, for a transitional period. The purpose is to ease the administrative burden on companies by abolishing all formalities prior to the movement of goods or related to the crossing of borders. Companies will instead have to keep fiscal and statistical records and make periodic declarations of any intra-EC commercial transactions to their national tax authorities.

To reduce the risk of tax evasion, increased administrative cooperation and exchange of information on VAT will have to be ensured among Member States.

Purchases of registered vehicles in another Member State and mail-order sales, under certain conditions, will be subject to VAT in the country of destination, at that country's prevailing rate, in order to maintain the neutrality of the common system of VAT.

A dilemma linked to the approximation of VAT and excise duty rates has been how to make it possible to introduce freedom of movement and support individuals' right to purchase while preventing excessive risks of distortion of competition. The proposed solution is that duty-free limits for travelers crossing EC frontiers will be abolished, beginning January 1, 1993. Because Denmark and Ireland fear a substantial loss of revenue to neighboring countries with lower rates, special arrangements may be made for them.

The problem of aligning VAT rates is far from being resolved. Member States are still at odds over the zero rate and the majority still favor a standard rate of 14 to 20 percent. On December 18, 1989, the Finance Ministers reached a compromise agreement on the narrowing of VAT rates which will postpone any changes until December 1, 1991, when new negotiations will be initiated to agree on a band or possible minimum rate. ECOFIN has until December 31, 1992, to decide on the scope of reduced rates for essential goods and services and to determine the products that may continue to be zero-rated.

Several other draft VAT directives are in the pipeline, some of which have been tabled, revived, and revised over many years. The 1985 White Paper announced a series of necessary, additional measures to achieve the completion of the EC's VAT base. There still are numerous variations and discrepancies among the VAT systems of the Member States, and the Commission's proposals are aimed at harmonizing the structure and range of these taxes.

10

Strengthening Monetary Cooperation and the European Monetary System

The European Commission stresses the need for increased cooperation on monetary policy and economic policy convergence. The creation of a financial area necessitates the reinforcement and development of exchange rate discipline and the participation of all the EC currencies in the exchange rate mechanism of the European Monetary System (EMS). The Commission sees the exchange rate mechanism (ERM) of the EMS and liberalization of capital movements as complementary. The latter cannot succeed unless there is financial stability.

THE EUROPEAN MONETARY SYSTEM

The EMS was established in March 1979. Its ERM is a currency system that assists the participant countries to achieve a greater degree of exchange rate stability against the other EC currencies.

Within the ERM, all the participating currencies have agreed exchange rates against each other. They are allowed to fluctuate above or below these central rates within bands of up to a maximum of 2.25 percent. The Spanish peseta, which recently joined the EMS, is permitted to diverge by up to 6 percent, and the Italian lira moved into the narrower band of 2.25 percent on January 5, 1990.

The question of UK membership in the EMS has been the subject of controversy and debate since its inception in 1979. The UK, which has for years been promising to become a full member of the EMS "when the time is right," is now the only major EC Member State that does not participate in the ERM. Spain joined the ERM in June 1989; nine out of the 12 Member States are now full members. Apart from the UK, Greece and Portugal are the only other Member States that are not full EMS members.

All 12 EC Member States are within the EMS through their respective currencies' involvement in the European currency unit (ECU). The ECU is a composite currency made up of all European currencies according to an agreed system of "weighting." It is enjoying increased usage in commercial banking transactions and in financial transactions between Member States, as well as by large corporations seeking to net out exchange rate variations in their European accounts. It would, of course, form the basis for the establishment of a true currency for the EC 12 if economic and monetary union (EMU) progresses. (See Appendix C.)

ECONOMIC AND MONETARY UNION

We discussed briefly in Chapter 1 the importance of EMU, the Delors report, and the significance of this issue in the debate between the United Kingdom and the European Commission on the future of the EMS. It is important to set out these issues and the substance of the Delors plan in more detail.

At the June 1988 Hanover Summit, the heads of state and government of the EC recalled that "in adopting the Single Act, the Member States confirmed the objective of progressive realization of economic and monetary union."

The Council decided to set up a Committee for the Study of Economic and Monetary Union, chaired by Jacques Delors, whose task would be "to study and propose concrete stages leading towards economic and monetary union."

In April 1989, "the Delors Committee" produced its *Report on Economic and Monetary Union in the European Community* ("the Delors report"). Three stages are identified as necessary for the achievement of monetary union. These are to be viewed as a single process and the report argues that a commitment to enter upon the first stage should be a commitment to undertake the whole process. The three stages recommended by the Delors Committee are described in turn.

Stage One

This stage would start by July 1, 1990, and would involve a strengthening of economic and monetary policy coordination within the framework of existing institutions.

- The Committee of Central Bank Governors would have a greater role in policy formulation and would be empowered to make recommendations to the Council and to the various governments on the monetary policies to be followed.
- All Member States would become full members of the EMS on equal terms.

The report recommends that the heads of state and government should decide before July 1, 1990 to call an intergovernmental conference charged with preparing, throughout this period, the changes in the treaties that would be required to set up the EMU. (The European Council, meeting in Strasbourg on December 8, 1989, agreed to convene an intergovernmental conference which will open at the end of 1990.) On March 12, 1990, the first steps toward EMU were taken. The Council of Finance Ministers adopted two decisions: the first dealing with the progressive convergence of economic policy and the second extending and reinforcing the tasks and rule of the Committee of Governors of the Central Banks of the Member States.

Stage Two

For stage two to be implemented, the treaty would have to be revised which would require the unanimous agreement of the Member States. During a transitional period, decision making in economic and monetary policy would be gradually transferred from national authorities to new institutional structures. A federal system under a European System of Central Banks (ESCB) would gradually be given responsibility for implementing European monetary policy.

Macroeconomic policy guidelines, including precise but not yet binding rules on the size of annual budget deficits in Member States, would be adopted. Fluctuation margins in the ERM of the EMS would be narrowed in preparation for stage three.

Stage Three

The final stage would begin with the irrevocable locking of exchange rates. Rules governing coordination in macroeconomic and budgetary policy would become binding. The EC would be empowered to interfere with national budgets. The ESCB would formulate and implement EC monetary policy. Reserves would be pooled and managed by the ESCB. National currencies would be replaced by a single currency. Economic and monetary decision-making powers would be transferred to the Council for economic questions and to the ESCB for monetary decisions.

The Delors Committee considers that the ESCB should be granted full status as an EC institution and should be autonomous and independent from national governments and other EC institutions. The ESCB's task would be fourfold:

1. Work toward price stability without financing the public debt of the Member States

2. Support the EC's general economic policy

3. Assume responsibility for monetary policy and management of exchange rates and reserves

4. Participate in the coordination of national authorities' banking surveillance

The ESCB would also have instruments at its disposal for taking action in the monetary sphere, such as the ability to intervene on the currency markets and the ability to buy and sell securities. It would have a federal structure and would consist of a council made up of the governors of Member State central banks appointed by the EC heads of state. The national central banks would have the task of implementing decisions taken by the ESCB.

The report does not propose a timetable for the progression from stage to stage; it gives only the deadline of July 1, 1990 for the initiation of the process of achieving monetary union. (On the same date, the directive for the full liberalization of capital movements takes effect.)

In line with the general decline of European cooperation through the 1970s, activity in the field of monetary integration was limited until 1979, when the EMS and the ECU were created. In Delors' report to the Madrid Summit he was able to note the following:

> Within the framework of the EMS the participants in the exchange rate mechanism (ERM) have succeeded in creating *a zone of increasing monetary stability* at the same time as gradually relaxing capital controls. The exchange rate constraint has greatly helped those participating countries with relatively high rates of inflation in gearing their policies, notably monetary policy, to the objective of price stability. [Committee for the Study of Economic and Monetary Union, *Report on Economic and Monetary Union in the European Community* (*The Delors Report*). Reprinted in Agence Europe 1550/1551, April 20, 1989.]

The report includes a discussion of the ECU's role and the need for *all* countries to join the ERM. (This latter reference applies, of course, to the UK.) At the Madrid Summit, Mrs. Thatcher set down the conditions under which she would allow sterling to join the ERM: the completion of the single market, the removal of all foreign exchange controls in the EC, the full implementation of a free market in financial services, and the strengthening of the EC's competition policy.

> If these conditions are met and provided inflation in the United Kingdom has been brought down significantly, the conditions would clearly exist to bring the pound into the exchange rate mechanism. (Margaret Thatcher, quoted in *European Report,* June 2, 1989)

If these conditions are met and sterling joins the ERM, stage 1 of Delors' three-stage plan to achieve EMU would be in place. The Delors report states clearly that the elements of monetary union are:

> —The assurance of total and irreversible convertibility of currencies;
>
> —The complete liberalization of capital transactions and full integration of banking and other financial markets; and
>
> —The elimination of margins of fluctuation and the irrevocable locking of exchange rate parties. [Committee for the Study of Economic and Monetary Union, *op. cit.*, p. 6.]

The final locking of exchange rates following sterling's involvement would conclude stage 1.

At Madrid in June 1989, however, Mrs. Thatcher argued that she did not feel stages 2 and 3 of the Delors plan were necessary or that they represented the only way forward on economic unity. Essentially the same stance was adopted in Strasbourg in 1989.

The UK's stance is very useful for highlighting some of the consequences of EMU for a Member State. The UK government is under considerable pressure to join the ERM. The Confederation of British Industry (CBI) and most other manufacturers and exporters are keen to join—a position not confined solely to export/import interests. By following this route and thereafter stages 2 and 3, Mrs. Thatcher, and all the other leaders, puts herself in the position of relinquishing control of interest rates and of fiscal policy. This prospect has sharpened her arguments against EMU. Her critics have pointed out that the use of interest rates and an aggressive monetarist stance has still left the UK with very poor inflation and unemployment figures compared to the other major European economies.

The other Member States, more anxious to move toward EMU, have hinted at going ahead without the UK if necessary. Issues such as taxation require unanimity but, as was pointed out in Chapter 1, the option is still open for the 11 Member States (exclusive of the UK) to sign an agreement outside the Treaty of Rome and the Single European Act. This eventuality was considered unlikely until late 1989, but the implications for non-European business's looking into a two-tier Europe, with the UK in the bottom tier, should be drawn—particularly in light of the new situation in Europe and the likelihood of a much expanded European structure, probably on two levels, in the next decade.

To American and Canadian ears the arguments surrounding EMU may seem exaggerated. Both the United States and Canada are federal systems: the federal government exercises limited control over the budgets of state or provincial legislatures. Speaking to the City University Business School in June 1989, Sir George Blunden, the deputy governor of the Bank of England, argued that the bringing together of economic policy could be achieved by means of agreement and permitted variations around a policy target, rather than by formal controls. The deputy governor pointed out that the creation of a monetary union comparable in size to the United States would "provide a strong impetus to whichever city was the union's main financial centre. London as the biggest centre in Europe would therefore have a strong claim to the operating centre of a European system of central banks" (*The Independent*, June 15, 1989).

It remains to be seen whether the UK will be in a sufficiently strong position to press London's claim when the time arrives.

III

OPPORTUNITIES FOR NON-EUROPEAN FIRMS

11

The View from Outside

The opening chapter of this book set out the political and economic framework in which the creation of a single market must be placed. The very foundations of the framework seem to shift daily as events in the Warsaw Pact countries continue to astound even the most seasoned observers. Subsequent chapters have set out the technical content of the single market program, particularly in financial services. This concluding chapter turns the perspective of analysis 180 degrees and seeks to assess the view from outside, or, more appropriately perhaps, to assess what outside observers should note or discard, to achieve the most effective interaction with the emergent Europe.

THE SPECTER OF "FORTRESS EUROPE"

Perhaps the most common fear expressed by outside observers is that, in creating the huge internal European market, the European Community is creating a "fortress Europe." This argument suggests that as the tariff walls come down within Europe, a tariff wall will be constructed on the EC's perimeter. European Commission officials have, of course, been quick to deny this but despite their many reassurances the fear still exists.

Fortress Europe as a threat or perceived threat grew out of fears that the financial services markets would be locked away from non-EC businesses. The solutions that have been reached on financial services do not take away the fortress Europe charge entirely. This issue is highlighted by the fact that whereas certain Member States are politically and philosophically committed to complete openness (the UK is a prime example in the financial services sector, notwithstanding strong regulatory procedures), other Member States are less than totally committed.

There can be no doubt that the effects of a single market on the peripheral economies of Greece, Portugal, and Ireland may be seriously damaging. The EC has already agreed to double the value of structural funds to these areas (plus parts of Spain and Italy) in recognition of this fact. Structural funds include the European Social Fund (for vocational training), the European Regional Development Fund (for infrastructure projects), and the Guidance section of the Agricultural Fund. In the months leading up to 1992 the bulk of these funds will be targeted at these "absolute priority regions," leaving little doubt that the funds represent anything other than a payoff for agreeing to commit these Member States to the Single European Act. The total sum involved in all structural funds will be 12,900 million ECU in 1993.

Recognizing the threat to some Member States and to certain key sectors in some of the advanced economies, some of the elected members of the European Parliament (MEP) have adopted a form of protectionist stance. The vast majority of MEPs accept the single market process as not reversible; some have begun to argue for temporary protective measures in some areas. In certain sectors where European industry is vulnerable, they say, specific protection should be afforded for a limited number of years. In some countries, industrialists will be pressing their MEPs to protect their interests by seeking to have special exemptions for their countries when certain directives come into force. But the EC will have to take great care if it enters those waters.

The EC is committed to its participation in various international trade agreements, in particular the General Agreement on Tariffs and Trade (GATT). Restrictions on trade, imposition of tariffs, and the like would in most instances be a flagrant contravention of GATT. In mid-1989, the EC's individual Member States operated about 730 quantitative restrictions on imports. Many of these were operated by Spain, Portugal, and other poorer economies under special exceptions. Ireland, Greece, Spain, and Portugal are often granted longer times to bring certain measures into effect. The United Kingdom too has enjoyed exemptions (such as the derogations referred to earlier in the book) from time to time on matters such as the size of axle weight loads for heavy trucks, water purification, and so on. These restrictions are being wound up and will stay in operation after 1992 only in exceptional circumstances.

As we have shown, the completion of the Single European Market (SEM) will make it impossible for any one Member State to restrict the import of a product from another Member State, no matter what the country or origin of that product. Entry to one EC Member State means entry to all 12. Those who would wish to protect a national champion industry from American or Japanese competition cannot do so unless the European border is made a barrier. To adopt this approach may serve immediate sectoral or short-term interests but will fly in the face of the philosophy of the single market program.

This is the philosophy of international free trade; its importance was demonstrated by the great sighs of relief that went up when the EC agreed on a final version of the second banking directive, which deals with reciprocity. In Chapter 5 the compromise position was explained, along with some of the continuing debate over the role of the various EC institutions in the enforcement and implementation of suspension. This revolves around the existing plan that a securities firm, for example, based in Paris could transact business in Madrid by reason of its French certification. If the Spanish rules with which the French firm must comply are breached, the Spanish authorities will investigate, but sanctions in the form of removal of certification will have to come from Paris. There are clearly some problems with this approach; not least is the need to comply with different sets of procedures and requirements. Financial services companies setting up within the EC will benefit from the reciprocity arrangements of the second banking directive but there is a lot to be done within the EC to finalize enforcement and regulatory procedures.

Any protectionism therefore will have to be on an EC-wide basis, and then the GATT antidumping measures can be brought into play by the EC. The European Commission has applied these in a number of interesting cases and they offer an indication of the machinery which the EC could use to protect key industries including, possibly, semiconductors and automobiles.

Reporting on a conference in London on the external implications of the single market, *Financial Times* remarked on two particular contributions. The first was by Johannes-Frederick Beseler, a senior Commission trade official who "brushed aside international fears that the single market would lead to an extension of national import restrictions to a Community wide level" (*Financial Times,* 24 July 1989). Beseler went on to argue that a wave of unprecedented liberalism in trade would be ushered in and even recognized that there may be trouble for some sectors in some Member States which Brussels would not be rushing to assist.

Beseler's speech obviously made little impression on a subsequent speaker, Kojiro Takano, from Japan's mission to the EC. Takano complained of the unreasonable local content requirements placed on Japanese products manufactured in third countries and argued that they were "legally unjustifiable, economically harmful and politically unwise." The classic example of Ricoh photocopiers was mentioned in this regard. Beseler maintained that the antidumping measures were applied in strict accordance with GATT. The argument that Europe had to protect itself against so-called Japanese "screwdriver" operations lay behind much of the exchange.

These, then, are the routes that the EC will have to take in the event that protectionism is seen as a means of supporting European industry: either specific exceptions for sectors or countries, or antidumping style tactics.

NON-EUROPEAN FIRMS PREPARE FOR 1992

What then is the current view from the outside? How are non-European business executives viewing the creation of a single market? Are Europeans about to find that the newly created market will be dominated by American, Japanese, and other non-European companies?

An increasing number of surveys and reports are being published on these questions. Among the more useful sources are: *Western Europe Regional Briefs* from the American Embassy in London; special reports by Booz-Allen Hamilton on Europe 1992 (1989); a report by the US Department of State on Europe 1992, *The Dynamics of Change;* and many reports and articles from leading European publications including *Financial Times, Eurobusiness,* and *Corporate Location Europe.* Readers are told that American businesspeople are preparing either very well, or not at all, for the prospect of Europe 1992. The reality seems to be that major international companies operating extensively in Europe regard it as a single market already and are well prepared for the prospect of the internal market. Major differences in attitude occur from sector to sector: new-technology sunrise industries show awareness and interest and are anxious to prepare, while others seek to defend their position or have no interest.

This defensiveness is a true sign of the times. Substantial transatlantic activity now operates in both directions as major European firms, especially UK operations, aggressively expand into North America.

The overall effect at all levels can be summed up in one word—*competitiveness.* Major restructuring is taking place in consumer durables. Deregulation in haulage and air transport, telecommunications, and other key sectors will result in fewer players on the European stage, far greater market share, and more effective research and development. It is no wonder that some non-European firms see the process as a threat rather than an opportunity. Much of this perceived threat is centered on the United States.

> More foreboding, but probably as accurate, over half of the US executives predict that European based firms will gain such strength from Europe 1992 efforts that they will be more effective competitors in the US. The bottom line: If American firms are unwilling to make the long-term investments needed to contend for new opportunities in Europe, they could wind up with a weaker domestic position as well. (*Europe 1992: Threat or Opportunity;* Booz-Allen Hamilton, 1989, page 7.)

The argument is supported by the increasing trade gap in Europe's favor as well as by the $158 billion cumulative direct investment from Europe into the United States—nearly 5 times the total Japanese figure.

We cannot easily forget, however, how deeply immersed in Europe the American business community has become. European subsidiaries of American companies employ 2 million people and often carry out development work and procure most of their materials and components locally. "We make in Europe more than 90% of what we sell here. Nobody else in our industry can make that statement," says Michael Armstrong of IBM. (Quoted in *Financial Times,* October 4, 1988.)

The contrast between perceived American and Japanese investment is important. American companies have supported EC local content and antidumping rules against Japanese companies. The Japanese, however, are rapidly moving in the same direction as the Americans. Achieving self-sufficiency within Europe is the key to not getting hurt.

Attention to Japanese investment has had a very high profile of late. Major investments in the UK by Nissan, Toyota, Fujitsu, and Matsushita (brand names: Panasonic, Technics, and National) reflect their response to Europe 1992. Locating within the EC immediately removes the consequences of any protectionism; locating in the UK brings not only substantial grant aid (probably available anywhere else) but also the support of Europe's most antiregulatory administration. The first Nissan off the production line in northeast England was driven off the ferry car transporter into France by the British Trade and Industry Secretary. Many factors affect the choice of strategy, once a company has located within Europe.

MAKING THE MOST OF THE NEW OPPORTUNITIES IN EUROPE

The Single European Market (SEM) will be a genuine and major opportunity for those who are ready to take it on. Anyone who currently exports into any one of 12 Member States knows that to export into the others requires yet another round of red tape for registration. After 1992 that will change. If a product is acceptable in one Member State it will automatically be acceptable in all 12. Bilateral certification agreements will have to be negotiated but they are in hand. Achieving entry will open up a market of 320 million consumers. The cost of developing an export market is clearly reduced. Small and medium size businesses, however, will have to keep track of directives, new specifications, and other information items relevant to their sector.

The single market is, of course, galvanizing business within Europe, and competition will become stiffer. The European Commission has developed a new commercial service to bring businesses together, a kind of "business marriage bureau" called Business Cooperation Network (BC-NET). As noted above, expanding European businesses will continue to look for suitable acquisitions on the American side of the Atlantic and this activity will increasingly happen among smaller companies. Conversely, American companies need to bring their European strategy onto the agenda and consider the implications of the unified market.

As we pointed out in Chapter 1, financial services sector deregulation means that lower cost providers in retail banking services will move into higher cost areas. At the retail level there is little prospect of much change in the national market places. Some Member States have very concentrated banking sectors and others are realigning rapidly, as in Spain. To gain broader representation across Europe, major European banks are repositioning.

> Interestingly in some instances (e.g., Deutsche Banks's purchase of the Bank of America's position in Italy) this repositioning includes capturing the retail positions of US banks that believe they can no longer respond to the pressures of the European harmonization process at the retail banking as opposed to commercial banking level. (*Europe 1992: Threat or Opportunity;* Booz-Allen Hamilton, 1989, page 26.)

Commercial banking, stock brokering, insurance, and all related fields are likely of course to concentrate in the unified market. The decision on where to locate has been made more complicated by the attempts of smaller cities to get a piece of the action. Not everyone wants to deal in London, Frankfurt, or Paris, or so some would argue. In Dublin, the Irish government has backed a major financial services development in a style reminiscent of the London Docklands development, although clearly on a smaller scale.

The very generous incentives (likely to be unacceptable in post-1992 Europe) include 10 percent corporation tax on profits, full remission of local taxation for 10 years, 100 percent capital allowances for commercial development, and double rent allowance against trading income. The tactic is, however, more likely to prevent migration of Irish asset financing, investment management, fund management, and similar activities to London, than to move non-Irish business to Dublin. The lesson is clear. In the financial services sector post-1992, peripheral regions and economies will have to fight to retain trade and standing.

Outside the EC but within Europe, the EFTA countries, including Norway, Sweden, Austria, Switzerland, and others, are reacting too. Some, notably Sweden and Switzerland are heavily linked into the EC market. Tactics by the EFTA governments vary. Austria lodged its application to join the EC in 1989 but Sweden favors seeking agreements on trade without full membership. This may be a model that the Commission would wish to consider, particularly in the light of the extraordinary political restructuring taking place in Eastern Europe. The process might also open a window for the Turkish application by providing the basis for a positive response without full commitment.

Third World countries too have major concerns. The new EC Member States of southern Europe (Spain, Portugal, and Greece) compete in the same agricultural markets as many of the 68 African, Caribbean, and Pacific states with which the EC has a trade and aid agreement. This agreement, the Lomé convention, allows free access to European markets for some key products in specific countries. For example, the removal of a guaranteed price for bananas may devastate the economy of

St. Lucia in the Caribbean. The consequences and implications of Europe 1992 are indeed many and varied.

To the professional accountant or solicitor offering advice on mergers and acquisitions in Europe, much of the above may appear irrelevant. Wide variations continue to exist in corporation tax, availability of information, rules relating to takeovers, management rights, accountancy practices, and so on. In the field of company accounts, for example, France has a central registration office for each of its 72 regions; obtaining company records becomes a lengthy process. However, French filing requirements and accounting standards ensure that detailed information is available to outsiders.

Attempting an acquisition in France is governed by takeover rules but the potential bidder should beware of the range of defensive measures which a management can deploy. In Germany a more difficult problem may be the degree of bank involvement in private firms. In the Netherlands, management rights make anything remotely hostile impossible.

Precisely because of this complexity there is one essential requirement for all business within and outside the European Community—planning. Even relatively small companies will be affected by the rapid pace of structural change currently going on in Europe. As major institutions and political bodies take on new roles and directions, their new positioning has a cascading effect into smaller scales of operation. The economies of Eastern Europe, despite having educated and highly trained but ill paid staff, have created an entirely new market situation in all fields, and not least in financial services. The push toward more rapid EC integration has been spurred further by President George Bush's comments to NATO allies following the Malta "nonsummit summit" with President Mikhail Gorbachev in 1989. The Strasbourg Summit in December agreed to establish the 1990 Intergovernmental Conference. Whatever the outcome of these major events, progress will continue on the single market program, and more and more of the directives outlined earlier will be implemented.

Companies looking to Europe need accurate and relevant information if they are to undertake the kind of detailed planning demanded by this complex situation. Traditional professional advisors may not have the most appropriate expertise in this instance. Strategic appraisal is also required to make sense of the shifting ground and to relate the detail of the single market to the particular requirements and direction of an individual business.

These, then, are the complexities that are changing Europe's economic landscape. Extensive work will carry on for years, to harmonize the production and distribution of resources. The implications are profound and far-reaching. Europe is now facing the challenge of creating the Single European Market while at the same time the greatest political restructuring since World War II creates new terms of reference at a staggering speed.

APPENDIXES

Appendix A

Measures Proposed and Adopted Relating to 1992 and Financial Services

(as of April 1990)

The following is a comprehensive list of relevant measures, classified under the headings in the European Commission's White Paper of June 1985. The list shows the current stage each individual proposal has reached in the decision-making process, along with appropriate document references. Copies of individual proposals and legislation can be obtained by contacting the nearest office of the European Commission (see Appendix E).

CONTENTS

3. *Creation of Suitable Conditions for Industrial Cooperation*
   - 3.1 Company Law
   - 3.2 Taxation
4. *Removal of Fiscal Barriers*
   - 4.1 VAT
   - 4.2 Excise Duties

ABBREVIATIONS USED

EP	European Parliament
ESC	Economic and Social Committee
OJL	Official Journal of the European Communities: Legislation
COM	Commission Document

Refer also to the List of Abbreviations on page xi.

For an explanation of EC legislative procedures, see Chapter 3.

Subject	*Document Reference*	*Status (As of April 1990)*
1. Financial Services		
1.1 Banks		
Bank Accounts Directive Directive 86/635 on the annual accounts and consolidated accounts of banks. Implementation required by 12/31/90. Rules to be applied to accounts 1/1/93.	COM(81) 84 Amended COM(84) 124 OJL 372 of 12/31/86	**Adopted 12/8/86**
Bank Branches Directive Directive 89/117 on the accounts of foreign branches of banks. Compliance by 1/1/91. To apply to annual accounts 1/1/93.	COM(86) 396 COM(86) 118 OJL 44 of 2/16/89	**Adopted 2/13/89**

MEASURES RELATING TO 1992 AND FINANCIAL SERVICES

Subject	*Document Reference*	*Status (As of April 1990)*
Mortgage Credit Services Directive Proposal for a directive on the freedom of establishment and the freedom to supply services in the field of mortgage credit.	COM(84) 730 Amended COM(87) 255	First reading
Winding-up Directive Proposal for a directive on the reorganization and winding-up of credit institutions and deposit guarantee schemes.	COM(85) 788 Amended COM(88) 4	First reading
Own Funds Directive Directive 89/299 on the harmonization of the concept of own funds. Implementation by 1/1/93.	COM(86) 169 Amended COM(88) 15 Amended COM(89) 208 OJL 124 of 5/5/89	**Adopted 4/17/89**
Deposit Guarantee Schemes Recommendation Recommendation 87/63 on the establishment of a guarantee system of deposit within the EC.	OJL 33 of 2/4/87	**Adopted 12/22/86**
Large Exposures Recommendation Recommendation 87/62 on monitoring and controlling large exposures by credit institutions.	OJL 33 of 2/4/87	**Adopted 12/22/86** Proposal for a directive to replace the recommendation expected to be submitted in 1990.
Second Banking Directive Directive 89/646 on the coordination of laws relating to credit institutions. Amends Directive 77/780. Implementation by 1/1/93.	COM(87) 715 Amended COM(89) 190 Amended COM(89) 621 OJL 386 of 12/30/89	**Adopted 12/15/89**

Subject	*Document Reference*	*Status (As of April 1990)*
Solvency Ratios Directive Directive 89/647 on solvency ratios for credit institutions. Implementation by 1/1/93.	COM(88) 194 Amended COM(89) 239 Amended COM(89) 578 OJL 386 of 12/30/89	**Adopted 12/18/89**
Recommendation 87/598 on a European code of conduct relating to electronic payments (relations among financial institutions, traders and service establishments, and consumers). Voluntary compliance by 12/31/92.	OJL 365 of 12/24/87	**Adopted 12/8/87**
Recommendation on Payment Systems Recommendation 88/590 on electronic payment cards: consumer protection.	COM(88) 427 OJL 317 of 11/24/88	**Adopted 11/17/88**
Consumer Credit Directive Directive 90/88, approximating the laws on consumer credit. Amends Directive 87/102. Implementation by 12/31/92.	COM(88) 201 Amended COM(89) 271 OJL 61 of 3/10/90	**Adopted 2/22/90**
Guarantees Regulation Proposal for a regulation on guarantees issued by credit institutions or insurance undertakings.	COM(88) 805	EP opinion delivered 2/14/90
Recommendation on Cross-Border Transfers Recommendation 90/109 on the transparency of banking conditions relating to cross-border financial transactions.	OJL 67 of 3/15/90	**Adopted 2/14/90**
Money Laundering Directive Proposal for a directive to make money laundering a criminal offense	COM(90) 106	Proposed 2/14/90

Subject	*Document Reference*	*Status (As of April 1990)*
1.2 Insurance		
Second Non-Life Insurance Directive Directive 88/357 to facilitate freedom to provide services in insurance other than life insurance. Implementation by 12/31/89 and 6/30/90 (transitional arrangements for Greece, Ireland, Spain, and Portugal).	COM(75) 513 Amended COM(78) 63 OJL 172 of 7/4/88	**Adopted 6/22/88**
Non-Life Framework Directive Proposal for a directive on non-life insurance, to include "mass risks"		To be proposed during first half of 1990
Legal Expenses Insurance Directive Directive 87/344 on coordination of laws relating to legal expenses insurance. Compliance by 1/1/90.	COM(79) 396 Amended COM(82) 43 OJL 185 of 7/4/87	**Adopted 6/22/87**
Credit Insurance Directive Directive 87/343 concerning credit insurance and suretyship insurance. Compliance by 1/1/90.	COM(79) 459 Amended COM(82) 255 OJL 185 of 7/4/87	**Adopted 6/22/87**
Insurance Contracts Directive Proposal for a directive on insurance contracts.	COM(79) 355 Amended COM(80) 854	No progress; possibility that proposal may be withdrawn
Winding-up of Insurance Companies Directive Proposal for a directive concerning the winding-up of insurance companies.	COM(86) 768 Amended COM(89) 394	EP favorable opinion 3/15/89
Accounts of Insurance Companies Directive Proposal for a directive on the annual accounts and consolidated accounts of insurance undertakings.	COM(86) 764 Amended COM(89) 474	First reading

Subject	*Document Reference*	*Status (As of April 1990)*
Third Motor Insurance Directive Proposal for a third directive concerning motor vehicle liability insurance.	COM(88) 644 Amended COM(89) 625	Common position adopted 12/15/89 EP second reading 2/4/90
Motor Insurance Services Directive Proposal for directive on freedom to supply services in the motor vehicle liability insurance sector (extends Second Non-Life Insurance Directive to include motor vehicle insurance).	COM(88) 791	EP opinion delivered 2/14/90
Second Life Insurance Directive Proposal for a directive on freedom to supply services in the field of life insurance. Amends Directive 79/267.	COM(88) 729 Amended COM(90) 46	Political agreement reached by Council 12/21/89
Life Framework Directive Proposal for further liberalization of life insurance ("mass risks").		To be proposed during second half of 1990
Pension Funds Directive Proposal for a directive on pension funds.		To be proposed during 1990
1.3 Transactions in Securities		
UCITS Directive Directive 85/611 for the coordination of laws, regulations, and administrative provisions regarding undertakings for collective investment in transferable securities (UCITS). Implementation by 10/1/89.	COM(76) 152 Amended COM(77) 227 OJL 375 of 12/31/85	**Adopted 12/20/85**
UCITS Amending Directive Directive 88/220 amending Directive 85/611 as regards the investment policies of certain UCITS.	COM(86) 315 OJL 100 of 4/19/88	**Adopted 3/22/88**

Subject	*Document Reference*	*Status (As of April 1990)*
Major Shareholdings Directive Directive 88/627 concerning information to be published when major shareholdings in a listed company are acquired or disposed of. Implementation by 1/1/91.	COM(85) 791 Amended COM(87) 422 OJL 348 of 12/17/88	**Adopted 12/12/88**
Prospectuses Directive Directive 89/298 coordinating the requirements for the drawing-up, scrutiny, and distribution of the prospectus to be published when securities are offered for subscription or sale to the public. Implementation by 4/17/91.	COM(80) 893 Amended COM(82) 441 OJL 124 of 5/5/89	**Adopted 4/17/89**
Amended Listing Particulars Directive Directive 87/345 amending Directive 80/390 to provide for mutual recognition of listing particulars. Due to enter into effect by 1/1/90.	COM(87) 129 OJL 185 of 7/4/87	**Adopted 6/22/87**
Prospectuses for Use as Listing Particulars Directive Proposal for a directive on mutual recognition of public offer prospectuses for use as listing particulars. Amends Directive 80/390.	COM(89) 133 Amended COM(90) 77	**Adopted 4/24/90**
Investment Services Directive Proposal for a directive concerning freedom to provide investment services.	COM(88) 778 Amended COM(89) 629	First reading
Capital Adequacy Directive Proposal for a directive on the capital adequacy requirements for investment firms.		Proposed

Subject	*Document Reference*	*Status (As of April 1990)*
UCITS Directive Jurisdictional clause.	COM(86) 193	Withdrawn (notice 7/21/88)
Insider Trading Directive Directive 89/592 on insider trading. Compliance by 6/1/92.	COM(87) 111 Amended COM(88) 549 OJL 334 of 11/18/89	**Adopted 11/13/89**
2. Capital Movements		
Directive 85/583 on liberalization of UCITS. Member States to take necessary measures to comply by 10/1/89.	COM(79) 328 OJL 372 of 12/31/85	**Adopted 12/20/85**
Proposal for a directive concerning the liberalization of transactions concerning mortgages.		To be proposed
Directive 86/566 for the liberalization of operations such as the issue, placing, and acquisition of securities representing risk capital, transactions in securities issues by EC institutions, and long-term commercial credit. Compliance by 2/28/87. Amends First Council Directive (1960) for the implementation of Article 67 of the EC Treaty.	OJL 332 of 11/26/86	**Adopted 11/17/86**
Directive 88/361 for the implementation of Article 67 of the EC Treaty (liberalization of capital movements) and also amending Directive 72/156 on regulating international capital flows and neutralizing their effects on domestic liquidity. Entry into force 7/1/90.	OJL 178 of 7/8/88	**Adopted 6/24/88**

Subject	*Document Reference*	*Status (As of April 1990)*
Council Regulation 1969/88 establishing a single facility providing medium-term financial assistance for Member States' balance of payments.	OJL 178 of 7/8/88	**Adopted 6/24/88**

3. Creation of Suitable Conditions for Industrial Cooperation

3.1 Company Law

Subject	*Document Reference*	*Status (As of April 1990)*
Proposal for a tenth directive concerning cross-border mergers of public limited companies.	COM(84) 727	EP has rejected proposals (held up over debate on fifth directive)
Eleventh Company Law Directive 89/666 to dispense branches of companies from publishing separate accounts.	COM(86) 397 Amended COM(88) 153 Amended COM(89) 528 OJL 395 of 12/30/89	**Adopted 12/21/89**
Proposal for a directive on the liquidation of companies.		Commission working party stage
Twelfth Company Law Directive 89/667 concerning single-member, private limited companies.	COM(88) 101 Amended COM(89) 193 Amended COM(89) 591 OJL 395 of 12/30/89	**Adopted 12/12/89**
Proposal for a Thirteenth Company Law Directive on takeover bids.	COM(88) 823	Proposal being redrafted
Further proposals to be made during 1990 aimed at removing legal obstacles to takeovers.		EP opinion delivered 1/16/90
Proposal for a Ninth Company Law Directive on the relationship between parent companies and subsidiaries.		To be proposed

Subject	*Document Reference*	*Status (As of April 1990)*
Regulation 85/2137 on a European Economic Interest Grouping. Compliance by 7/1/89.	OJL 199 of 7/31/85	**Adopted 7/25/85**
Proposal for a Fifth Company Law Directive (structure of public limited companies).	COM(72) 887 Amended COM(83) 185	First reading
Proposal for a regulation on a European Company Statute and a directive complementing the statute with regard to the involvement of employees in the European company.	COM(70) 600 Amended COM(75) 150 Amended COM(88) 320 Amended COM(89) 268	First reading
Proposal for a directive amending Directive 78/660 on annual accounts and Directive 83/349 on consolidated accounts with respect to the exemptions for small and medium-size companies.	COM(86) 238 Amended COM(88) 292	ESC opinion published 3/31/89
*3.2 Taxation**		
Arbitration procedure concerning the elimination of double taxation.	COM(76) 611	No progress
Proposal for a directive concerning a common system of taxation applicable to parent companies and their subsidiaries.	COM(69) 6 Amended COM(85) 360	Blocked over problem concerning Germany's withholding tax
Common system of taxation of mergers, divisions, and contributions of assets.	COM(69) 5	No progress

* Removing tax obstacles to cooperation among enterprises in different Member States.

Subject	*Document Reference*	*Status (As of April 1990)*
Harmonization of taxes on transactions in securities. Superseded by proposal to abolish taxes on securities transactions.	COM(76) 124 Amended COM(87) 139	ESC and EP have given opinions
Harmonization of Member States' laws relating to tax arrangements for carryover of losses of undertakings.	COM(84) 404 Amended COM(85) 319	No progress
Proposal for a directive on a common system of withholding tax on interest income.	COM(89) 60	Blocked; revised guidelines produced
Proposal for a directive amending Directive 77/799 concerning mutual assistance by the competent authorities of the Member States in the field of direct taxation and VAT.	COM(89) 60	Council reached agreement on a compromise text 12/18/89
4. Removal of Fiscal Barriers		
4.1 VAT		
Proposal on special VAT schemes for small business (includes flat-rate farmers' proposal now no longer necessary).	COM(86) 444 Amended COM(87) 524	Not yet adopted
Proposal for 12th VAT Directive concerning expenditure on which tax is not deductible.	COM(82) 870 Amended COM(84) 84	Not yet adopted
13th VAT Directive 86/560 concerning tax refunds to persons not established in the EC. Entry into force 1/1/88.	COM(82) 443 Amended COM(83) 413 OJL 326 of 11/21/86	**Adopted 11/17/86**

Subject	*Document Reference*	*Status (As of April 1990)*
Proposal for 16th VAT Directive concerning imports by final consumers of goods that have already borne tax in another Member State.	COM(84) 318 Amended COM(86) 163	Not yet adopted
17th VAT Directive 85/362 concerning the temporary importation of goods other than means of transport. Entry into force 1/1/88.	COM(84) 412 OJL 192 of 7/24/88	**Adopted 7/16/85**
18th VAT Directive 89/465 concerning the abolition of certain derogations [Article 28(3)] of Directive 77/388.	COM(84) 649 Amended COM(87) 272 OJL 226 of 8/3/89	**Adopted 7/18/89**
Proposal for 19th VAT Directive: miscellaneous supplementary and amending provisions of Directive 77/388.	COM(84) 643 Amended COM(87) 315	Not yet adopted
Proposal for a Directive completing the common system of VAT and amending Directive 77/388. Approximation of VAT rates.	COM(87) 320 Amended COM(87) 321 Amended COM(89) 260	New guidelines on VAT approximation 6/14/89 Council compromise agreement 12/18/89
Proposal modifying 6th VAT Directive (77/338) so as to treat sales and purchases across intra-EC borders in the same way as those within Member States; the removal of fiscal barriers.	COM(87) 322	Revised proposal 5/17/89
Proposal on passenger transport.	COM(87) 322/2	To be proposed

Subject	*Document Reference*	*Status (As of April 1990)*
Proposal concerning the establishment of a VAT clearing house system (working document produced 1987).	COM(87) 323/2	To be proposed
Proposal for a directive instituting a process of convergence of rates of VAT and excise duties (replaces standstill proposal on both VAT and excise duties).	COM(87) 324	ESC opinion published 9/12/88
Proposal for a directive on the stores of ships, aircraft, and international trains.	COM(79) 794	Not yet adopted
Proposal for a directive amending 6th VAT Directive—special arrangements for second-hand goods, works of art, antiques, and collectors' items.	COM(88) 846	Not yet adopted
4.2 Excise Duties		
Proposal concerning harmonization of the structure of excise duties on alcoholic drinks.	COM(72) 225 Amended COM(85) 150 Amended COM(85) 151	No progress
Decision 88/245 concerning harmonization of the structure of excise duties on alcoholic drinks.	COM(82) 153 OJL 106 of 4/27/88	**Adopted 4/19/88**
Proposal concerning the harmonization of the structure of excises on mineral oils.	COM(73) 1234	No progress
Proposal concerning the final stage of the harmonization of the structure of cigarette duty (rates and system).	COM(87) 325 Amended COM(89) 525	ESC opinion published 9/12/88 EP move to reject proposal 3/28/89

Subject	Document Reference	Status (As of April 1990)
Proposal concerning the approximation of taxes on manufactured tobacco products, other than cigarettes (tax rates and system).	COM(87) 326 Amended COM(89) 525 COM(89) 551	ESC opinion published 9/12/88 New proposals on excise duties for tobacco, alcohol, and mineral oils
Proposal for common rate bands for harmonized excise duties on mineral oils.	COM(87) 327 Amended COM(89) 526	ESC opinion published 9/12/88
Proposal for common rate bands for all harmonized duties on alcoholic beverages.	COM(87) 328 Amended COM(89) 527	ESC opinion published 9/12/88 EP move to reject proposal 3/22/89

Appendix B

Commissioners and Directorates-General

The European Commission is made up of 17 Commissioners, each with a particular portfolio of responsibility. The Commissioners include two from each of France, Germany, Italy, the United Kingdom, and Spain, and one from each of the other countries. A new Commission was appointed in 1989; its members will serve for four years. They are:

Jacques Delors (France), President of the Commission	Monetary affairs
Karel van Miert (Belgium)	Transport Credit, investments, and financial instruments Consumer protection
Henning Christopherson (Denmark)	Economic and financial affairs Coordination of structural instruments Statistical office
Christiane Scrivener (France)	Taxation Customs Union Questions relating to obligatory levies
Vasso Papandreou (Greece)	Social affairs and employment Education and training Human resources

Ray MacSharry (Ireland)	Agriculture Rural development
Filipo Pandolfi (Italy)	Research and science Telecommunications Information technology and innovation Joint research center
Carlo Ripa di Meana (Italy)	Environment Nuclear safety Civil protection
Jean Dondelinger (Luxembourg)	Audio-visual policy Cultural affairs Information and communications Citizens' Europe Office for Official Publications
Frans Andriessen (Netherlands)	External affairs and trade policy Cooperation with other European countries
Antonio Cardoso e Cunha (Portugal)	Personnel and administration Energy Euratom Supply Agency Policy on small and medium-size enterprises Tourism Social economy
Manuel Marin (Spain)	Fisheries Cooperation and development
Abel Matutes (Spain)	Mediterranean policy Relations with Latin America North–South relations

Leon Brittan (United Kingdom)	Competition Financial institutions
Bruce Millan (United Kingdom)	Regional policy
Martin Bangemann (West Germany)	Internal market and industrial affairs Relations with the European Parliament
Peter Schmidhuber (West Germany)	Budget Financial control

The Commissioners are served by the 23 Directorates-General of the European Commission and by a Secretariat-General, a Legal Service, a spokesperson's service that is directly under the authority of the President of the Commission, a Joint Interpreting and Conference Service, and a statistical office.

The Commission also funds a European Foundation for the Improvement of Living and Working Conditions, based in Dublin, and a European Center for the Development of Vocational Training (CEDEFOP), based in Berlin. The Commission maintains information offices in all the Member States and external delegation offices in more than 90 countries including the United States (Washington, DC and New York, NY), Japan (Tokyo), Canada (Ottawa), Brazil (Brasilia), Syria (Damascus), India (New Delhi), and so on. These delegations are very pleased to receive enquiries and to provide information.

The 23 Directorates-General are organized essentially as departments and are:

I	External Relations
II	Economic and Financial Affairs
III	Internal Market and Industrial Affairs
IV	Competition
V	Employment, Social Affairs, and Education
VI	Agriculture
VII	Transport

VIII	Development
IX	Research and Administration
X	Information, Communications, and Culture
XI	Environment, Consumer Protection, and Nuclear Safety
XII	Science, Research and Development
XIII	Telecommunications, Information Industries, and Innovation
XIV	Fisheries
XV	Financial Institutions and Company Law
XVI	Regional Policy
XVII	Energy
XVIII	Credit and Investments
XIX	Budgets
XX	Financial Control
XXI	Customs Union and Indirect Taxation
XXII	Coordination of Structural Policies
XXIII	Enterprise Policy

More information on any of these departments can be obtained from the EC's delegations in the various countries or by telephone from the Commission offices in Brussels (Brussels 235 11 11). The caller will be answered by one of the most multilingual groups of telephonists employed anywhere.

The European Commission department responsible for drawing up the proposals in the financial services program is Directorate-General XV (DG 15), Financial Institutions and Company Law.

Appendix C

The European Currency Unit (ECU)

The ECU is the official monetary unit of the European Community and forms a part of the European Monetary System (EMS).

It is used as:

1. A unit of account; it is not a hard currency, although a commemorative coin has been produced. The ECU is legal tender in Belgium.
2. A reserve instrument
3. A basis for calculating exchange rate divergences

The ECU is composed of all of the currencies of the Member States. Its composition was reviewed in September 1989 to take account of the inclusion of the Spanish peseta and the Portuguese escudo. The new weightings are:

Deutsche mark	30.1%	Spanish peseta	5.3 %
French franc	19.0	Danish krone	2.45
Pound sterling	13.0	Irish punt	1.1
Italian lira	10.5	Greek drachma	0.8
Dutch guilder	9.4	Portuguese escudo	0.8
Belgium franc	7.6	Luxembourg franc	0.3

(Figures do not exactly total 100% due to rounding.)

The amount of each currency is determined by:

- Each Member State's GDP, relative to the others
- The contribution to trade within the EC

The amounts remain constant until reviewed by the European Banking Association (EBA). A review takes place every five years; the next is due in September 1994.

CURRENCY WEIGHTING

Weighting of each currency will vary, in percentage terms, with changes in the value of each national currency in the foreign exchange market. However, there are fixed limits on this variation. If any weighting moves by more than 25 percent in the five-year period, a Member State can call for an early review of the currency amounts that make up the ECU.

Currency variations in the weightings of the ECU are further limited by the Exchange Rate Mechanism (ERM), part of the European Monetary System (EMS). Under the ERM, national currencies are not allowed to diverge from the central rate fixed by the EMS by more than 2.25 percent (6 percent Spanish peseta). These limits do not apply to the pound sterling, Portuguese escudo, or Greek drachma, which are not included in the ERM.

Although it has not yet occurred, should any national currency begin to diverge by more than 75 percent of its maximum limit under the ERM, the national government authority responsible would be expected to act to correct the fluctuation by:

1. Intervening in foreign exchange markets,
2. Altering domestic monetary or fiscal policies, or
3. Asking for a new central rate and weighting.

Thus the ECU has been established within the EC as a currency of account that is relatively stable and liable to minimum fluctuations against most individual EC currencies.

USES AND CHARACTERISTICS OF THE ECU

Availability

The ECU has become widely available and acceptable as a means of settlement and a unit of account in international transactions. Some companies are also finding trading partners outside the EC who are willing to quote in ECUs rather than dollars, because of the latter's volatility.

Recognition

All central banks in the EC recognize the ECU and acknowledge it as a fully fledged European currency.

Use by Governments

The ECU has become the means for settling accounts among monetary authorities in the EC, although a central bank need take only a maximum of 50 percent of any receipt in ECU if it wishes.

Use for Financing International Investment

Because the ECU is weighted strongly in favor of the presently low-cost Deutsche mark, the cost of borrowing in ECUs is comparatively cheaper than many other national currencies. Coupled with its relative stability in value, this has made the ECU an attractive medium for international investment. The European

Investment Bank (EIB) issues public loans in ECU and the ECU is also used by the European Development Fund.

Simplification of Treasury Management

Multinational companies with extensive European operations can use the ECU to reduce currency risk and simplify their treasury management operations. Such companies often have customers and suppliers in different EC countries. By arranging payments and receipts in ECUs, currency exposure in EC member currencies can be reduced and lower currency management costs result.

Internal Accounting in One Currency

Companies with several subsidiaries in different EC countries can organize internal accounting and transfer pricing within the group more easily, if intragroup business is conducted in ECUs.

THE FUTURE OF THE ECU

Although a unified European currency may not be imminent, the ECU has real potential to become a key trading currency. Certain industrial groups have formed an Association for the Monetary Union of Europe which aims to encourage the use of the ECU in international trade.

Other proposals to boost the ECU include:

- EC national governments' procurements to be priced and invoiced in ECUs
- Joint projects among national organizations within the EC to account in ECUs

- All commodities wholly produced and consumed in the EC to be denominated in ECUs

Supporters of monetary union argue that the evolution of a single European currency can only help in competition against the other major trading blocks of the US and Japan, which do not have the hindrance of many different currencies.

Appendix D

Bibliography

The material used in the compilation of this book has been taken from primary sources of EC documentation produced by various European Commission institutions. Listed below is a selection of publications providing useful background information. See Appendix E for a list of institutions that can provide copies of these and other useful documents and publications.

ON THE GENERAL THEME OF 1992

Budd, Stanley. *The EEC: A guide to the maze,* 2nd ed. London: Kogan Page, 1987.

Cecchini, P., et al. *The European challenge—1992: The benefits of a single market.* Aldershot: Wildwood House, 1988. (A brief synoptic paperback version of the complete report, referred to below.)

Commission of the European Communities. *The big European market: A trump card for the economy and employment,* European File, 14/88, August/September 1988.

______. *Communication from the Commission on implementation of the legal acts required to build the single market,* COM(89) 422 final. Brussels, September 1989.

______. *Europe without frontiers—a review halfway to 1992,* European File, 10/89, June/July 1989.

______. *Completing the internal market: An area without internal frontiers. Report on the progress required by Article 8B of the Treaty,* COM(88) 650 final. Brussels, November 1988.

______. *Completing the Internal Market: White Paper from the Commission to the Council,* COM(85) 310 final. Brussels, June 1985.

______. *The Economics of 1992,* European Economy, No. 35, March 1988.

______. *Europe 1992: Developing an active company approach to the European market.* London, 1988.

______. *First Report from the Commission to the Council and the European Parliament on the implementation of the Commission's White Paper on the completion of the internal market,* COM (86) 300 final. Brussels, May 1986.

______. *Fourth Progress Report of the Commission to the Council and the European Parliament concerning the implementation of the Commission's White Paper on the completion of the internal market.* Brussels, June 1989.

______. *Making a success of the Single Act: A new frontier for Europe,* COM(87) 100 final. Brussels, February 1987.

______. *Research on the Cost of Non-Europe.* Luxembourg, Office for Official Publications of the European Communities, 1988. 16 Volumes. ("The Cecchini report")

______. *Second Report from the Commission to the Council and the European Parliament on the implementation of the Commission's White Paper on the completion of the internal market,* COM (87) 203 final. Brussels, May 1987.

______. *The Single Act: A new frontier for Europe,* Bulletin of the European Communities, Supplement 1/87, 1987.

______. *The Single European Act,* Bulletin of the European Communities, Supplement 2/86, 1986.

______. *Target 1992: Europe without frontiers: Towards a large internal market,* European File, 17/87, November 1987.

______. *Third Report from the Commission to the Council and the European Parliament on the implementation of the Commission's White Paper on the completion of the internal market,* COM(88) 134 final. Brussels, March 1989.

______. *Europe without frontiers—completing the internal market,* European Documentation, 3/1988 (2nd edition), February.

On the Single Financial Market

Commission of the European Communities. *The creation of a European financial area: The liberalization of capital movements and financial integration in the Community,* European Economy, No. 36, May 1988.

_____. *A European financial area: The liberalization of capital movements,* European File, 12/88, June/July 1988.

_____. *Global Communication from the Commission on the completion of the internal market: Approximation of indirect tax rates and harmonization of indirect tax structure,* COM (87) 320 final. Brussels, August 1987.

_____. *Research on the Cost of Non-Europe,* Volume 8, Luxembourg, Office for Official Publications of the European Communities, 1988.

_____. *Towards a big internal market in financial services,* European File, 17/88, November 1988.

Committee for the Study of Economic and Monetary Union. *Report on Economic and Monetary Union in the European Community (The Delors Report).* Reprinted in Agence Europe 1550/1551, April 20, 1989.

Servais, D. *The Single Financial Market.* Brussels, Commission of the European Communities, 1988.

Other Sources of Information

In addition to the published sources listed in the bibliography, the interested reader may wish to know of information centers that can be contacted directly by telephone.

The originators of this book, Spicers Centre for Europe, have offices in most of the EC Member States. In addition there is a New York Spicers Centre for Europe.

Contact: Tom Phillips
or: Kathy Edersheim
Spicers Centre for Europe
Spicer & Oppenheim
7 World Trade Center
New York, NY 10048

Tel: (212) 422 1000
Fax: (212) 669 6996

The headquarters of Spicers Centre for Europe is the United Kingdom office in Leeds.

Contact: Paul Quantock
or: Jenny Lawson
Spicers Centre for Europe
10-12 East Parade
Leeds
West Yorkshire LS1 2AJ
United Kingdom

Tel: (0532) 442629
Fax: (0532) 449909

There is also a Spicers Centre for Europe in Wellington, New Zealand.

Contact: Morgan D. Pierce
Spicers Centre for Europe
Spicer & Oppenheim
3rd Floor CMC Building
89 Courtenay Place
PO Box 6549
Wellington 1
New Zealand

Tel: (04) 845939
Fax: (04) 859237

The European Commission has information offices in all EC Member States. The main center is, of course, Brussels. A query should relate to one of the areas of responsibility associated with the Directorates-General listed in Appendix B. The European Commission at Brussels is a large organization; relevant address is:

The European Commission
Rue de la Loi 200
1049 Brussels
Belgium

Tel: (02) 235 1111
Fax: Various fax numbers depending on section and Directorate-General

The telephone receptionists in Brussels are possibly the most linguistically versatile anywhere. English speakers will have no difficulty in gaining access to a suitable official if they persist.

The European Commission has offices in the following locations:

United States of America

Head of Delegation
2100 M Street, NW (7th Floor)
Washington, DC 20037

Tel: (202) 8629500
Fax: (202) 4291766

Head of Delegation
3 Dag Hammarskjold Plaza
305 East 47th Street
New York, NY 10017

Tel: (212) 371 3804
Fax: (212) 758 2718

Canada

Head of Delegation
Office Tower
Suite 1110
350 Sparks Street
Ottawa, Ontario KIR 7S8

Tel: (613) 238 6464
Fax: (613) 238 5191

Japan

Head of Delegation
Europa House
9-15 Sanbancho
Chiyoda-KU, Tokyo 102

Tel: (03) 2390441
Fax: (03) 2615194

Australia

Head of Delegation (also responsible for New Zealand)
Capital Centre
Franklin Street
PO Box 609
Manuka ACT 2603
Canberra

Tel: (062) 955000
Fax: (062) 953712

In addition to the delegations to non-EC states, the European Commission has developed a hierarchy of information centers in association with national and university libraries and research centers in Europe and around the world. These include:

- European Documentation Centers (EDC). There are 300 of these worldwide, usually based in academic institutions. They are intended to encourage academic research and teaching. Some receive all official documentation, others have received only a selection since a review of usage in 1987/1988.
- EC Depository Libraries (DEP). These are major collections of EC documentation intended for use by the public.
- European Reference Centres (ERC). These are collections of basic documentation, usually in academic institutions. Key documents are available but ERCs are a limited resource.

A list of EDCs, DEPs, and ERCs is provided below for the United States, Canada, Japan, Australia, and New Zealand.

Only the name of the key institution is given. For a specific person's name at that institution, contact the delegation office of that country or Directorate-General X in Brussels.

The following abbreviations are used in the list:

EDC	European Documentation Center receiving comprehensive supply of EC documentation
EDC(S)	EDC receiving basic EC documentation plus material from a selection of prechosen policy areas
DEP	EC depository library
DEP(R)	EC depository library receiving a selection of EC documentation
ERC	European Reference Center

EC Information Centers

	Source and Location	*Information Key*
Australia		
Bundoora	La Trobe University	EDC
Canberra	National Library of Australia	DEP(R)
Hobart	University of Tasmania	EDC(S)
Melbourne	State Library of Victoria	DEP(R)
Nedlands	University of Western Australia	ERC
Sydney:	German-Australian Chamber of Industry and Commerce	ERC
	State Library of New South Wales	DEP
	University of Sydney	EDC(S)
Canada		
Burnaby	Simon Fraser University	ERC
Charlottetown	University of Prince Edward Island	ERC
Downsview	York University	ERC
Edmonton	University of Alberta	ERC
Fredericton	University of New Brunswick	ERC
Halifax	Dalhousie University	EDC(S)
Kingston	Queen's Univerity	EDC
Moncton	Université de Moncton	ERC
Montreal:	McGill University	EDC (English)
	McGill University	EDC(S) (French)
	Université de Montréal	EDC(S)
Ottawa:	Bibliothèque Nationale du Canada	DEP(R)
	Carleton University	EDC
	University of Ottawa	ERC
St. Catherine's	Brock University	ERC
Ste. Foy	Université Laval	
St. John's	Memorial University of Newfoundland	ERC
Saskatoon	University of Sakatchewan	ERC
Sherbrooke	University of Sherbrooke	ERC
Sudbury	Université Laurentienne	ERC

EC Information Centers

	Source and Location	*Information Key*
Toronto	University of Toronto	EDC
Vancouver	University of British Columbia	ERC
Waterloo:	Wilfried Laurier University	ERC
	University of Waterloo	ERC
Winnipeg	University of Manitoba	EDC
Wolfville	Acadia University	ERC
Japan		
Fukuoka	Seinan Gakuin University	EDC
Fukuyama	Fukuyama University	EDC(S)
Hokkaido	Otaru University of Commerce	ERC
Ishikawa	Kanazawa University	EDC(S)
Kagawa	Kagawa University	EDC(S)
Kawauchi, Sendai	Tahoku University	EDC
Kyoto	Doshisha University	EDC
Nagoya:	Nagoya University	EDC(S)
	Nanzan University	ERC
Okinawa	University of the Ryukyus	EDC
Osaka	Kansai University	EDC(S)
Saitama	Saitama University	ERC
Sapporo	Hokkaido University	EDC(S)
Shizuoka-Ken	Nihon University	EDC(S)
Tokyo:	Chuo University	EDC
	Keio University	EDC(S)
	National Diet Library	DEP
	Sophia University	EDC(S)
	University of Tokyo	EDC
	Waseda University	EDC(S)
New Zealand		
Auckland:	Auckland Public Library	DEP
	University of Auckland	EDC(S)
Christchurch	University of Canterbury	EDC
Wellington	Parliamentary Library	DEP(R)

EC Information Centers

	Source and Location	*Information Key*
United States		
Albany	State University of New York at Albany	DEP
Albuquerque	University of New Mexico	DEP
Ann Arbor	University of Michigan	DEP
Athens	University of Georgia	EDC(S)
Atlanta	Emory University	DEP
Austin	University of Texas	DEP
Berkeley	University of California	DEP
Bloomington	Indiana University	DEP
Boulder	University of Colorado	DEP
Buffalo	State University of New York at Buffalo	DEP
Cambridge	Harvard Law School	DEP
Champaign	University of Illinois	DEP
Charlottesville	University of Virginia	DEP
Chicago:	Library of International Relations	DEP
	University of Chicago	DEP
Columbia	University of South Carolina	DEP
Columbus	Ohio State University	DEP
Durham (North Carolina)	Duke University	DEP
East Lansing	Michigan State University	DEP
Eugene	University of Oregon	DEP
Evanston	Northwestern University	DEP
Gainesville	University of Florida	DEP
Honolulu	University of Hawaii	DEP
Iowa City	University of Iowa	DEP
La Jolla	University of California	DEP
Lawrence	University of Kansas	DEP
Lexington	University of Kentucky	DEP
Lincoln	University of Nebraska	DEP
Little Rock	University of Arkansas	DEP
Los Angeles:	University of Southern California	DEP
	University of California	DEP

EC Information Centers

Source and Location		Information Key
Madison	University of Wisconsin	DEP
Minneapolis	University of Minnesota	DEP
New Haven	Yale University	DEP
New Orleans	University of New Orleans	DEP
New York:	Council on Foreign Relations	DEP
	New York Public Library	DEP
	New York University	DEP
Norman	University of Oklahoma	DEP
Pennsylvania	Pennsylvania State University	DEP
Philadelphia	University of Pennsylvania	DEP
Pittsburgh	University of Pittsburgh	DEP
Portland	University of Maine	DEP
Princeton	Princeton University	DEP
St. Louis	Washington University	DEP
Salt Lake City	University of Utah	DEP
Seattle	University of Washington	DEP
South Bend (Indiana)	University of Notre Dame	DEP
Stanford	Stanford University	DEP
Tucson	University of Arizona	DEP
Washington:	The American University (CERDEC)	EDC
	The Library of Congress	DEP

Index